Simple Weaving

Simple Weaving

Designs
Material
Technique

Grete Kroncke

 VAN NOSTRAND REINHOLD COMPANY
New York   Cincinnati   Toronto   London   Melbourne

Van Nostrand Reinhold Company
Regional Offices:
New York Cincinnati Chicago
Millbrae Dallas
Van Nostrand Reinhold Company
International Offices:
London Toronto Melbourne

This book was originally published
in Danish under the titles *Sjove
væveformer* and *Sjove Med Tov*
Høst & Søns, Forlag, Copenhagen,
Denmark

Library of Congress Catalog Card
Number # 72-7846
ISBN 0 442 29972 9 cl
ISBN 0 442 29981 8 pb

Translated from the Danish by
Christine Hauch
Photography — Bull Foto
This book is printed in Great Britain
by Jolly & Barber Ltd. Rugby
and bound by Henry Brooks, Cowley, Oxford.

Published by Van Nostrand
Reinhold Company Inc.
450 West 33rd St., New York,
N.Y. 10001 and Van Nostrand
Reinhold Company Ltd.,
25-28 Buckingham Gate,
London SW1E 6LQ

Published simultaneously in
Canada by Van Nostrand
Reinhold Company Ltd.

16   15   14   13   12   11   10   9   8   7   6   5   4   3   2   1

Contents

Introduction

The author has chosen to concentrate on two aspects of simple weaving rather than to write a general introductory text. The first section, 'Looms with a difference', demonstrates some very basic ideas for looms; apart from one single exception they are all home made and can be built very cheaply. Examples include a card loom, a bow loom, a cycle wheel loom and a plank loom.

The reader is shown how various articles can be made on such looms but the emphasis is really on the 'machines' and weaving techniques rather than the output.

'Making string things' is the second section and shows the work which can be done with cord and twine. The qualities of cord and twine vary enormously according to the raw materials used to make them up and the results which can be achieved differ as widely. Sisal, jute, hemp, cotton twine and paper string are all used to decorate and make a large range of objects, from bottles and jars to handbags and spectacle cases.

The demands on resources in both sections of the book are very modest and although not underestimating some of the problems involved in the work, the author hopes that her ideas will be possible for all.

LOOMS WITH A DIFFERENCE

Forked branch used by Navaho Indians to make a primitive form of ribbon loom. Ethnographical department of National Museum of Denmark.

A few words about weaving techniques

Weaving consists of two groups of threads at right angles to each other. One of these is known as the *warp*. This is stretched tight across the loom. The weft (also called woof) is the thread which is interlaced with the warp (see figure A).

The most simple form of weaving is called *plain weave* (or tabby). In plain weave the warp and weft are equally visible in the woven work which is also called the web. Plain weave is produced by alternately raising and dropping every other warp thread, thereby making a so-called shed. Through this is inserted the weft thread. The next weft thread is passed through a shed created by raising and dropping the opposite threads.

The *shed* can be made in various ways. You can, for example, use a *heddle* threading the warp threads alternately through slit and eye. When the loom has been threaded up or dressed by stretching the warp over it, sheds are made by first lifting then lowering the heddle. The weft, which is wound onto a shuttle, is inserted alternately from the right and left sides of the web as each shed is made.

A

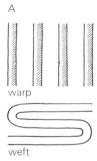

warp

weft

B

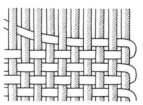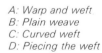

A: Warp and weft
B: Plain weave
C: Curved weft
D: Piecing the weft

C

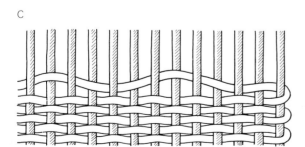

D

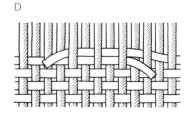

On more primitive looms one shed is made by lifting a preferably flat *pick-up stick* and the other by pushing back the stick and lifting the opposite threads. There are various ways of doing this and the method for each loom in the section is described in the relevant chapter.

It is important to weave, that is to insert the weft thread, without pulling the outer thread of the warp too tight or making the whole warp too taut (see figure C where the weft is interlaced in curves).

Piece the weft as shewn in figure D by allowing the threads to run side by side for about 1-1½ inches (3-4 cm). The ends can be cut off later. Attach the weft in the same way.

If one of the warp threads breaks you can join it with a weaver's knot to a new thread which is drawn through the reed and fastened (see figure E). Fastening off the warp is done as follows: cut the web from the loom about 4-8 inches (10-20 cm) from the last weft thread according to the length of the fringe. Knot two or more warp threads together and tighten right up to the last weft thread.

E: Weaver's knot which can be used to piece the warp.

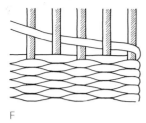

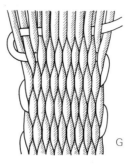

F

G

H

If you don't want a fringed web, cut it off the loom about 4 inches (10 cm) from the last weft thread and darn the warp back into the work. Alternatively you can secure the ends with a row of close machine stitching. A cushion cover could be made in either of these ways for example.

F: Weft rep
G: Warp rep
H: Twill weaving

Other weaves

Weft rep: here only the weft threads are visible (see figure F).
Warp rep: except for the small loops at the edge only the warp threads which create the pattern, are visible. This can be used with a ribbon loom (see figure G).
Twill weave is woven over two and under two threads and shifted along one thread on each row. Use this weave with a plank loom (to give one idea), since it creates a firmer fabric (see figure H).

Most looms use shuttles to insert the weft. You can saw a shuttle from a flat piece of wood which is well sandpapered down. For small looms the shuttles can be cut out of thick cardboard.

For some of the looms in this book you will want a very thick, blunt needle instead of a shuttle through which to thread the weft. For just one of the looms, the plank loom, we have used a long upholstery needle with an upturned point. Like the shuttle the needle is also used to press the weft together. You can also employ a comb or a tapestry beater, a reed or, if it is flat on one side, the shuttle. Note the different tools in figure I.

I

1
2
3
4
5

I: Various additional tools. 1 and 4 shuttles, 2 pattern stick, 3 pick-up stick and 5 upholstery needle.

11

Card loom

The little card loom in the picture is the simplest form of loom. It is so easy to use that even the youngest child can learn to weave on it.

It consists of a piece of stiff cardboard with squared paper glued on the ends so that notches can be cut at regular intervals without difficulty.

The *warp* thread, which is stretched over the card, can either be wound right round the board catching it in the notches at each end or drawn across the front and behind a notch, so that on the back the warp looks like 'stitches' from notch to notch (see diagram).

The actual weaving is done by darning over and under the warp with a long, blunt needle.

You can make a pattern by, for example, inter-changing the colours you are darning with, to achieve a striped effect.

By this method you can make such objects as small carpets for dolls' houses and dolls' bags. You can also use a card loom to make small samples before embarking on a larger piece on a big loom.

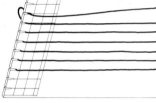

Dressing a card loom. Notice the squared paper which makes it easy to cut notches at regular intervals.

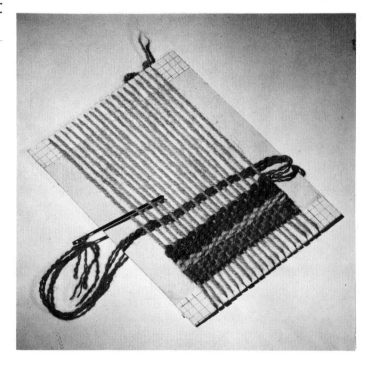

Card looms can be used for samples, but dolls' house carpets, purses and so on can also be woven on them.

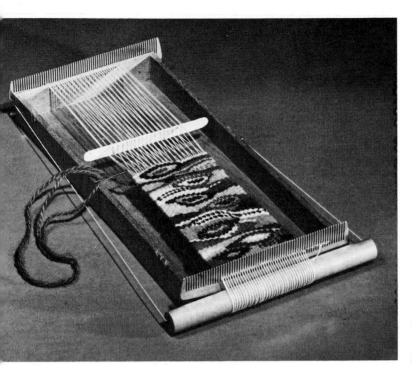

With two combs and a cigar box you can make an unusual and handy little loom ideal for trying out new patterns and materials or, as here, for weaving a small picture big enough for a spectacle case or a purse.

Cigar box loom

This very simple form of loom is basically made of a cigar box and two combs, though if you haven't a cigar box you can make a similar loom from pieces of wood. A big cigar box, about 12 inches (30 cm) long, can be used to weave something the size of a spectacle case. Using a needle as here instead of a shuttle, you can also do tapestry work. Obviously different size boxes can be used. The models in the first section of the book provide more of a format than a prototype.

Making the loom. The two combs in this model are made of metal but other combs can be used provided they are strong and even, that is to say that there is the same distance between the teeth. Glue the combs firmly to the ends of the cigar box with Araldite or some other strong all-purpose glue, taking great care that they lie exactly opposite each other.

If you are using pieces of wood instead of a cigar box join them to form a frame onto which the combs can be glued.

Dressing the loom. To secure the end of the warp, which in this case is twine, weave it in and out of the teeth on one side of the comb, as shewn on the right side of the front comb in the photograph.

You may feel it would be good to be able to pull the warp tight. For this purpose a solid cardboard roll can be inserted as in the photograph. Bind this roll tightly to the loom. A piece of wood between this roll and the cigar box will help to tighten it.

Then wind the warp right round the cigar box making sure that the thread passes through the teeth of each comb which lie directly opposite one another. When the warp is of the required width — that is the width intended for the finished article — the end of the thread can be secured in the same way as at the start.

Insert an iced lolly stick or a wooden spatula (of the kind used by doctors which can be bought at any chemist) so that it lies alternately over and under the threads. Then you can make a shed by lifting the stick as shewn in the picture. Now darn the thread in at right angles.

Use a needle instead of a shuttle as mentioned above.

Various kinds of yarn of different thicknesses have been used for the web in the picture. The ends are on the wrong side. The tapestry technique allows you to weave oblique lines, for example to make ovals as here.

The same technique as shewn here can also be used on other of the looms in the book, or on completely different looms. You just have to make sure that you have a comb for the warp, or a comb-like utensil such as a piece of wood with closely and carefully sawn notches.

Bow loom

This simple form of loom is often to be found in museums and in books about primitive cultures. It consists of a flexible branch bent into a bow with the threads, which make up the warp, stretched between the two ends of the bow. The weft is then darned or woven through the warp in one or more colours according to the pattern.

Making the loom. We have used a willow branch for this loom but other kinds of wood can also be used provided they are pliable enough. Bend the branch carefully until you have the required span, then tie the two ends to hold this arc (see figure 2). Drill a hole at each end with a $\frac{1}{16}$ inch drill so that the hole goes across the string. If the branch is very thick enlarge the hole with a wider drill afterwards.

Preparation of the warp. Make the warp of wool or cotton yarn. You can either make it the exact length between the ends of the bow so that the internal tension keeps it stretched or allow a greater length and bind it round the set of shed rods on which the warp is made. This will mean that the finished work can be longer than the bow.

The warp is made over four small sticks which are pulled tightly together in pairs. This can be done as here, for example, by setting the sticks in two vices with the required distance between them

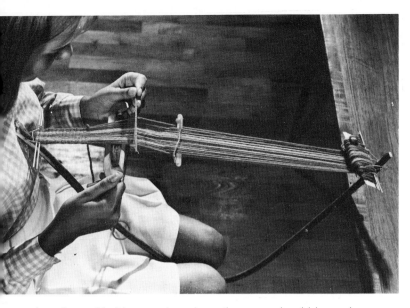

2. The bow loom is a distinctive form of loom made of a bent branch, on which bands of different widths can be simply and easily produced.

(see figure 3). Measure how long the warp should be and you can make it plain coloured or in three colours for a striped pattern as here. Wind the various colours in the order you wish round the shed rods.

When changing to another colour you can either break off the thread and knot it to the next colour or let the ends hang loose and bring them into play again later when you next wish to use that colour. If you want to make a symmetrical pattern you should dress the loom from one side into the middle and from there to the other side using the same colours in the reverse order.

When the warp is finished tie the shed rods together in pairs so that the warp cannot slip off. If the warp has been made longer than the space on the loom wind the surplus round one pair of rods.

Tie the shed rods to the bow with strong twine stuck through the holes drilled at the ends (see figure 4).

3. Preparation of warp for bow loom and others.

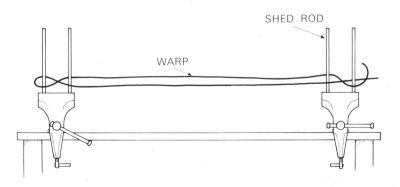

SHED ROD

WARP

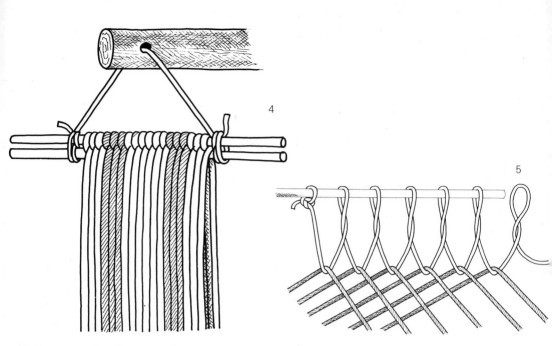

4

5

4. The two small rods hold the warp threads in the right order.

5. This shows how you can make one shed by passing loops of thread down round alternate warp threads and up round a little stick while the other shed is made by lifting the small, flat pick-up inserted over and under alternate warp threads.

Once the loom has been dressed you can ensure that you have the correct tension.

Making the shed. To be able to weave you need to be able to make two sheds. *The first* is made by a light stick and thread. Draw a loop round every alternate warp thread and up round the stick as in figure 5. Continue the whole width of the warp. *The second* shed is made by a small flat stick like an iced lolly stick. Make a little hole in each end of the stick, push it through the warp threads alternately over one and under one making sure that it lies over the thread pulled up by the loop on the other stick. Tie a string across the flat stick to hold it in place and position it behind the first stick. See the picture on page 15.

The weft is wound round a shuttle or threaded in a blunt needle. Place the bow of the loom firmly between the knees supporting the back against a table and the front against your body. Now start weaving in the ordinary way: alternately lift the loops and insert the shuttle through the resulting shed and lift the flat stick behind it to form the second shed through which the shuttle can be passed from the opposite side.

Make sure that the tension on the weft is uniform so that the edges remain even and the width stays the same throughout. If your warp is longer than the loom, roll it gradually onto the shed rods at one end as the unworked warp is rolled off the rods at the other end. It is easiest to weave with cotton yarn or some similar material which doesn't make too much fluff.

Cycle wheel loom

With this particular form of loom you can achieve unusual results since the weaving process is carried out in a circle, making the end product circular. The size of the finished article will obviously be limited but even the dimensions of a cycle wheel allow for many possibilities. We show three different ideas but with a little imagination you will doubtless be able to come up with even more.

It is not specially difficult to get hold of a cycle wheel. If you don't own an old bicycle yourself which you could dismantle you can try asking a bicycle dealer for an old wheel. It should preferably be fairly big. Remove the spokes and if the wheel is rusted and dirty wash it clean and sandpaper it. Cover the rim well with paint in a bright colour which will go with whatever you are intending to weave; then the wheel will be attractive to look at as well.

In the rim you will find the spoke holes plus one where the valve has been, making an odd number altogether. When the paint is dry,

Cycle wheel loom.
Below the finished rag rug and above the round wall hanging which can be seen in colour on the cover.

17

number these holes by starting with the hole next to the valve hole and writing the numbers on the outer edge of the rim. You will then end with the valve hole giving it the highest odd number. This system of numbers will enable you to dress the loom. You will find it easiest to use gummed labels.

The warp can be single or double thread depending on how thick it is and what the end product is intended to be. Be careful not to make the web too thick in the middle if it is meant to lie flat on the floor. A slightly prominent point in the centre may, however, add interest to a wall hanging.

The length of the warp is reckoned by measuring the diameter of the wheel and adding the extra piece needed to pass the thread into the hole from outside along to the next hole and out again as in figure 6. Multiply this length by the number of times the warp has to cross from one side to the other, i.e. the number of holes divided by two since each crossing of the thread involves two holes. Over and above this length (which includes half the diameter for the last hole) you should reckon on about one yard extra for shrinkage and for starting the weaving in the centre. If you want a double warp (as in the case with the round wall hanging and the sun thistle) dress the loom with double thread.

Dressing the loom. This must be done in one particular way or the thread will be incorrectly distributed and you won't finish in the valve hole.

On the cycle wheel we have used there are 36 spoke holes plus the valve hole. In this case the loom is dressed as follows: start by tying on the thread at hole 19 and passing it over to hole 1 where it is introduced from the outside (as in figure 6) and then to hole 2. From there the thread goes to 20 and 21 and then in the following order:

hole	3-4	over to	22-23
,,	5-6	,,	24-25
,,	7-8	,,	26-27
,,	9-10	,,	28-29
,,	11-12	,,	30-31
,,	13-14	,,	32-33
,,	15-16	,,	34-35
,,	17-18	,,	36-37

Then guide the thread in towards the centre and down between numbers 19 and 20 before bringing it back to hole 37 as shewn in figure 7. By this method the threads are held fast. Pull the end tight and make sure that the intersection lies exactly in the centre.

Now you can start weaving by *interlacing* the rest of the warp thread. In most cases you will find it useful to weave the first little piece over two and under two warp threads, or over four and under four if a double warp is being used. Take the final thread singly, however, since this kind of interlacing requires an uneven number of warp threads. Continue with this method for a few inches and

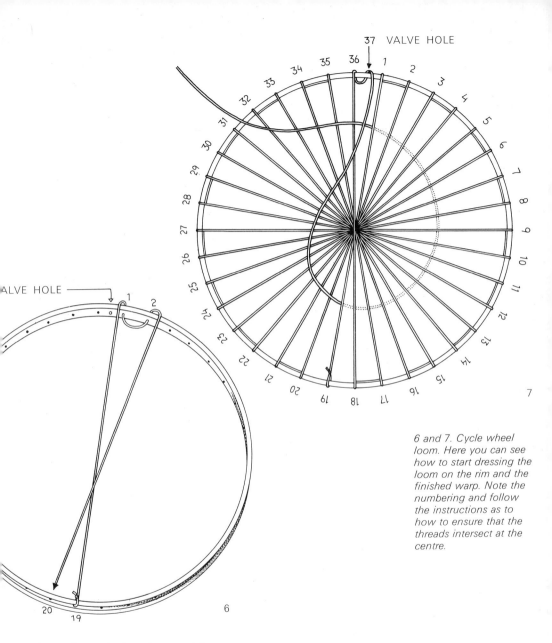

*6 and 7. Cycle wheel
loom. Here you can see
how to start dressing the
loom on the rim and the
finished warp. Note the
numbering and follow
the instructions as to
how to ensure that the
threads intersect at the
centre.*

then take each thread separately.

If the wheel is of a different size or has a different number of holes you would be as well to draw a circle on which you can mark and number the holes. Then you can keep tabs on your progress by drawing pencil lines on your diagram before you start dressing the loom.

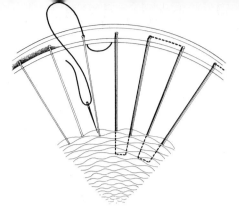

8. Setting in the extra warp which is used when the existing warp thread is very thick but the central intersection should not be too bulky.

Small rugs

Use a really strong yarn for the warp, but since it is so thick it should be threaded singly.

The weft is composed of coloured rags torn into suitable strips from stockings and underclothes together with other remnants. Apart from different kinds of cloth you can use thick wool or cotton yarn, perhaps plying several thicknesses of yarn, twine, string, raffia or all kinds of things. This is an excellent opportunity for using up various kinds of remnants. *Interlace the weft with your fingers.*

Weave a small piece and then introduce extra warp threads in the following way: tie a thread the same thickness as the warp to the rim and draw it down along side the warp into the web for a couple of inches and back along the next warp thread (see figure 8). Continue in this way right round the loom until the whole warp has been doubled. The new thread should be tight but not drawn so tightly that the web shrinks. After introducing the extra warp divide the threads as you weave so that you go over and under one at a time.

Cycle wheel loom. Here is an old cycle wheel with the spokes removed to form an unusual circular loom.

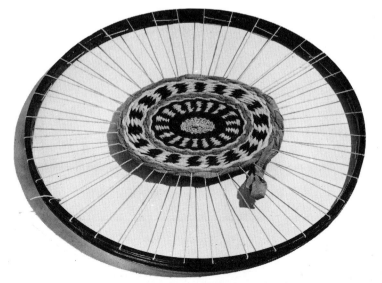

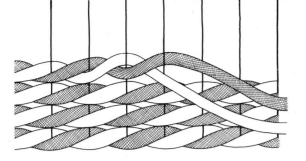

9. Cross weaving with
rags or thread.

For ordinary weaving you use an odd number of warp threads but when making a pattern which is striped out from the centre you should have an even number. This can be achieved by weaving the threads from holes 36 and 37 together. This way you can either weave a row alternately with one colour then the other or braid the two weft threads in a kind of cross weaving (see figure 9). This technique, however, will work best at the outer edge of the web where the warp threads are more widely spaced.

Finish off the work a little way from the rim and cut the threads at the outer edge between the holes. Pull the warp out of the holes and sew the ends in on the back of the web. If the ends are 'uncontrollable' you can knot them in pairs and fasten them with a little blob of glue.

Mount the web on a piece of carpet underlay (rubberized), cut to the same size and edge with tape. Attach the web to this by stitching round the edge and possibly in the centre if required.

Round wall hanging

Dress the loom with a double warp and use various red, orange and mauve shades of wool with odd rows of raffia now and again for the weft. Weave the wool over two warp threads in the centre, then divide the warp after about 4 inches (10 cm) and weave over and under one thread to achieve a tighter weave. Here you can introduce more, and possibly thicker, threads by twisting them into the work with a cross weave. Make sure that the tension is tight enough to prevent bulges but loose enough to stop the edges contracting when the web is removed from the loom.

Before removing the web cut a piece of cardboard exactly the same size. When the warp threads have been cut tie them in pairs right in at the edge of the web. This is easiest if you do it thread by thread, cutting and tying as you go. Finally, glue the ends to the back of the cardboard and cover this in turn either with a piece of material or another piece of board backed with material. Then fix a cord to the back by which to hang it on the wall.

Sun thistle

This wall hanging is woven in yellow, flame and orange wools.

10. Diagram of the procedure for interlacing in the spaces between the woven work.

Dress the loom with a sisal warp as described for the round wall hanging. After weaving about $1\frac{1}{2}$ inches (4 cm) leave a small piece of the warp unworked. You can return to this piece later. Continue in this way until you are a few inches from the rim. Then go back to the gap nearest the centre and interlace two double threads. Divide the warp at the next gap so you are interlacing two single threads (see figure 10).

When finishing off at the outer edge, interlace two threads as before but make sure that the warp threads leading to the same hole are drawn together (see figure 10). Use a needle for this process.

When the web is finished cut it off the loom and secure the ends. You will achieve a really decorative effect if you leave the sun thistle on the wheel and hang the whole piece up. You will probably find it easy enough to get hold of another cycle wheel the next time you want to weave in this way.

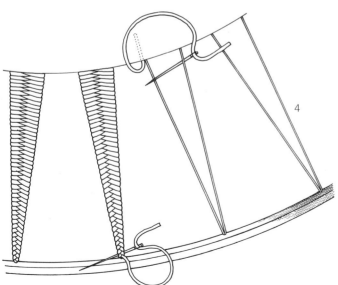

Cycle wheel loom. You can either leave the sun thistle on the wheel, as here, or remove it. In the latter case you should weave a metal ring into the outer ring of true weaving and fasten the ends in with glue or by darning to retain the circle. Weave the sun thistle in yellows, oranges and reds.

22

Plank loom

Some years ago, while travelling in Holland I heard that the people of Volendam had special looms, called plank looms, which they used to weave the scarves that go to form their characteristic regional costume.

On visiting Volendam I was allowed, after some discussion, to buy a plank loom — 'It is usually something you make yourself!' I also bought a scarf and was given a short course of instruction in the use of the loom. Nowadays these looms are mostly used for the quick production of rough scarves for tourists. But you can still buy the original scarves which when worn as part of the regional costume are folded lengthwise, put around the neck and down in front.

The loom I bought consisted of an old board with rusty nails in.

By working on the basic idea and developing it, I was able to make the loom easier to work with and to provide opportunities for varying the length and width.

I applied the same idea to a smaller but broader loom (see figure 11) which can be used to weave such articles as bags, cushion covers, and napkins, and which also has the advantage of being

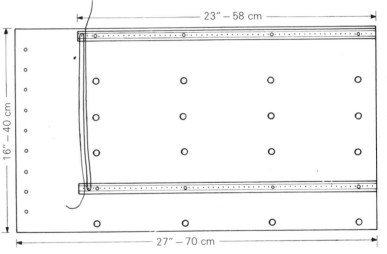

11. Small plank loom suitable for bags, napkins etc.

Plank loom 1. The great thing is to work out which finger position will make the darning process most comfortable. The picture shows clearly how the threads are kept separate by the large nails. Note the tapestry beater.

Plank loom 2. You will need plenty of room at each side for this long loom since you will find it most restful to move the loom along as you work. The little plank loom in figure 11, on the other hand, is extremely easy to sit at and may be a great comfort if you are stuck in bed.

convenient to work with if you are confined to bed. Both the short and long looms have been introduced with some success into occupational therapy courses.

Unlike most proper looms, such as frame looms and other large looms, dressing the plank loom is quick and easy. It only needs one person, which means a great deal to whoever intends to start weaving.

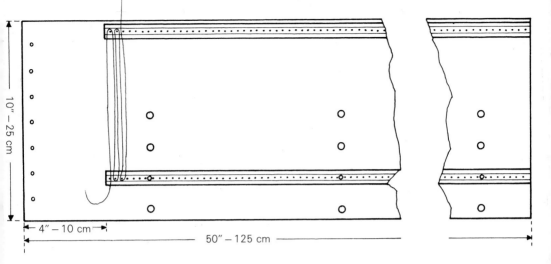

10" – 25 cm

4" – 10 cm

50" – 125 cm

Before going any further it should be said that this is not a conventional loom. For one thing you cannot make a shed in the warp but must darn in the weft with an upholstery needle (see picture).

12. Large plank loom with beginnings of warp, though this is usually threaded double.

Making a plank loom. The loom can be varied in length (compare figures 11 and 12) but the method does not vary at all. Fasten two pieces of wood to the plank, the length and shape indicated in the diagrams. One of these should be removable. Drill a row of holes along the plank through which to insert the screws which will ensure that you can take one of the pieces of wood off the board. You will be able to keep the movable piece at the correct distance from the edge by using wing nuts underneath. The scarf will be as wide as this distance.

If you drill several rows of holes you will be able to move the piece of wood to different distances from the edge. So, one of the advantages of using this kind of loom is that you can make articles of various widths on the one loom.

At the same time you will find it easier to darn in the weft because the warp is raised from the surface of the plank. Bang small, headless nails into the pieces of wood about $\frac{1}{2}$ inch (1 cm) apart. You can glue squared paper on first to make sure that the nails are equally spaced. Knock about 6-8 larger nails along the ends of the plank as in figure 13. Attach rubber studs to the underside so that the screws don't scratch the table. You may want to make the back studs

13. Plank loom seen from one end. The large nails keep the threads in their respective positions as you darn them in.

25

slightly higher so that the loom is tilted and more comfortable to work with. In that case you should attach the studs a little way in from the edge, since that side of the loom is used to wind the weft threads round (see figure 14).

Dressing the loom. Using one continuous thread, pass the warp across from nail to nail, as in figure 11. As a rule you should use a double warp, slipping a finger between the two threads as you dress the loom to prevent them twisting together. Be sure to keep the tension even all the way along, as the warp tends to be too loose especially at the ends.

In some cases you will find that the underside of your sleeves catches on the nearest row of nails as you work so it may be useful to cover these. The simplest way to do this is with plastic spines which you can buy at a stationers. They are usually used to keep several pieces of paper together, but can easily be slipped over the nails. They will also prevent the warp threads from coming off.

Wind the weft yarn round one long side of the plank (see figure 14) and cut at one end. When darning in the weft you should use a long upholstery needle with an upturned point.

Use of the web. This size loom is particularly suited to the weaving of scarves but can also be used to produce other articles, for example bags, table mats, cushion covers by simply threading a shorter stretch of warp.

14. The darning process. Note how the weft threads are divided and pushed out to the side.

Darning. Thread two, three or four of the pieces of yarn you have cut, depending on the thickness of the yarn and how coarse you want the finished article, and draw them through the needle so that the ends are together. As a rule it is best to weave the first few rows

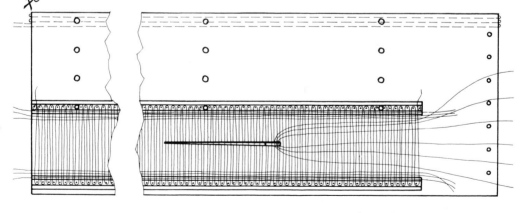

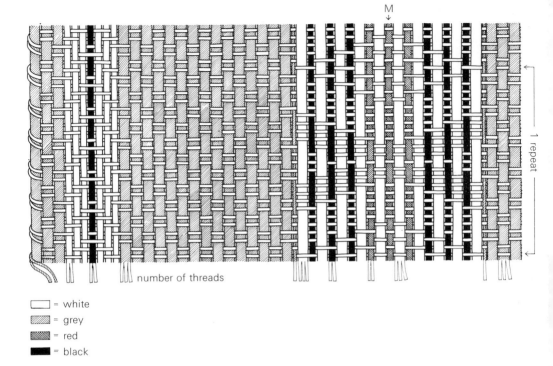

M
↓

1 repeat

number of threads

☐ = white
▨ = grey
▦ = red
■ = black

in the same material as you have used for the warp, but otherwise there is no reason why you should not use odds and ends of yarn as long as they are the right length and colour.

If you have a double warp weave the two first rows alternately over and under two threads to fix the warp to the nails and make a firm edge. When you have inserted the needle a little way put the threads into the right order and arrange them between the nails at the end of the plank. You will now be able to pull the needle through without the threads becoming jumbled. When you have pulled the threads right through, cut them by the eye of the needle, divide them and push each half out to the opposite sides with a comb. Make sure that these threads are loose so that they don't tauten the web.

Darn in the next row over and under the opposite threads, but after that you are free to use your imagination and come up with all kinds of patterns (see figure 15). You can make a small test piece by just threading the warp a little way along the end with the large nails. This way you will be able to practise the darning technique and work out how thick and closely woven you want the finished article.

When the web is finished you can adjust the ends slightly and arrange the fringing before removing the work from the loom. The easiest way to do this is by sewing round a suitable number of threads and into the web with a kind of hem stitch.

Finally ease the web from the nails; possibly you will need to

15. Diagram for weaving of a scarf on a plank loom.

Scarf woven on a plank loom. The ground is ordinary plain weave. The warp is grey yarn used double. The borders are woven as shewn with three threads of soft yarn in the colours of the pattern. Make the pattern symmetrical by weaving along the middle and pushing the threads out to each side.

loosen the movable piece of wood. If you want to make the fabric fluffy and the yarn you have used is suitable, dampen it thoroughly and brush it backwards and forwards diagonally with a stiff nail brush.

A small plank loom

A small loom is well suited to the weaving of short wide articles. It is easy to work with and, as we have already mentioned, convenient to use in bed, especially if the plank is of a light weight wood. You could make a small loom to measure 16 by 28 inches (40 by 70 cm). For example (see figure 11). Drill the rows of holes through which to fasten the extra pieces of wood 2 inches (5 cm) apart.

Scarf and handbag woven on a plank loom. The scarf is woven on a long loom. The warp is plain coloured but the weft is composed of several colours to make stripes. The bag has been woven in the same colours on a small loom. Both articles have been dampened and brushed with a hard nail brush to finish them.

Ribbon weaving and darning on a rigid heddle

I have decided to include the technique of ribbon weaving on a rigid heddle for various reasons although it is the only 'loom' in the book which has not been home made.

It is constructed in accordance with the same principle as many of the old valve looms you can find in museums around the country. These were sewn from a thin, flat piece of wood, often with delicate patterns worked into one side. This side was curved and fitted with a hole from which to hang the loom up when not in use. You could make a similar loom yourself, sawing it out of plywood, for example.

One of the main reasons why it is included here is because it is easy to use and cheap and thus very suitable for beginners.

With this kind of weaving you can make ribbon, ties, belts, narrow scarves, sample pieces and, when using the heddle as a darning loom, small woven pictures.

Ribbon weaving

1. Make the warp either by winding the thread round the edge of a tabletop, over a coat rack or in the usual way with sticks.
   Lay the thread on a table and place something heavy over the warp so that the loops are free.
2. Clamp a width holder to a table so that the small holes are accessible. Stand the heddle in front of this with the support of two shed rods through the large holes. Draw the loops of thread of the warp one by one through the slits of the heddle and then through every other hole on the holder. Keep the loops in place by hooking them over a knitting needle or shed rod behind the holder as in figure 17. Make sure that the warp is centred in the heddle. Remove the weight. Then pull the heddle slowly towards the other end of the warp until you have the length you want for the finished article.
3. Cut the loops in the warp in front of the heddle. Thread whichever of the two threads in the slit is meant to go through the eye with a crochet work.

16. Rigid heddle with the tools for ribbon weaving and darning.

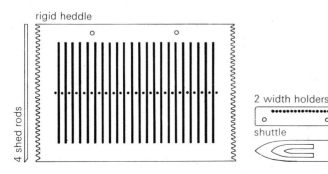

4 shed rods · rigid heddle

2 width holders

shuttle

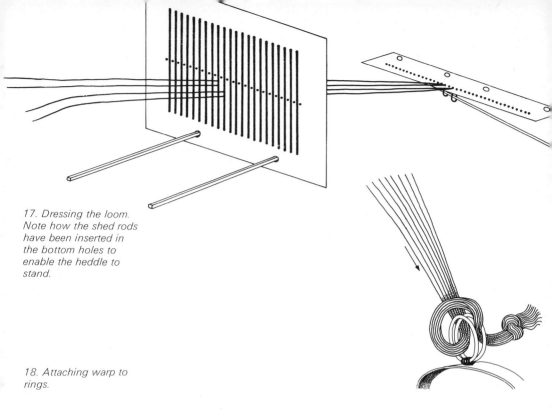

17. Dressing the loom.
Note how the shed rods
have been inserted in
the bottom holes to
enable the heddle to
stand.

18. Attaching warp to
rings.

4. Pull the threads till they are equally taut and tie in a knot.
5. Attach two rings or buckles firmly to a belt or a firm border (see figure 18).

   Tie the belt round your waist with the rings in front. Then pull the warp threads up through both rings and back under the back one. You can then control the tension of the warp by moving your own body backwards.
6. Wind the weft thread round a shuttle and you are ready to start weaving.

   You make the shed through which to introduce the weft by raising and sinking the heddle, which you can also use to beat the work. To ensure that the edges are even you can loop the weft thread over a finger while you pull it through (see figure 19).
7. The quality of the strip of weave is controlled entirely by the weaving process, with the warp thread showing and the weft thread virtually invisible. The rule is that the warp threads should lie so close together that they are almost touching.

Weaving the full width

1. Set the warp in the same way as described but instead of knotting them all together, divide them into groups of about six threads and then tie them (see figure 20).

30

2. Draw a piece of strong string through the hole farthest to the right on the width holder and tie it tight. Pass the string up through the righthand group of warp threads and back through the sixth hole on the holder, on through the next group of threads, back into the twelfth hole and so forth until all the threads have been loosely attached to the holder. Then tie the string fast in the farthest hole to the left.

19. Weaving on a ribbon loom.

20. Weaving the full width. Here the work has been fixed to a belt with buttons and loops.

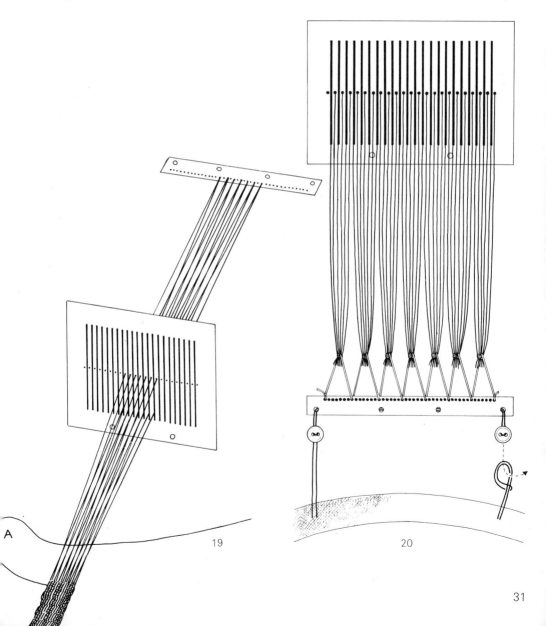

A

19

20

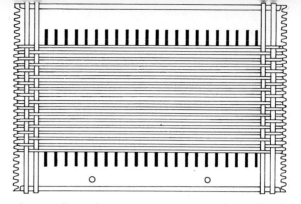

21. The loom used as a darning frame.

3. Thread an ordinary button onto a strong piece of string. Draw both ends of string through the large hole on the right of the holder, up through the hole on the left and thread another button to this end of the string. Tie the ends of the string so that the buttons hang about ¾ inch (2 cm) from the holder.
4. Make two loops about 4 inches (10 cm) long and sew them into the belt about 7 inches (18 cm) apart. Slide these loops over the buttons with a running loop as in figure 20. It is important that the warp be tautened as little as possible while weaving.
6. Make the shed as described with the heddle, using it as a beater for the weft also.

Roll the finished web round the holder as you go by passing the buttons and loops out to the sides and turning the entire holder once with the top edge in towards the web. After you have rolled the work on put the buttons and loops back in place *up* over the edge of the holder so that the latter is locked in place. If the holder bends too much the tension of the warp is too tight. You can always stiffen the holder by pushing a knitting needle through the wound up threads but this should not be necessary.

Darning

If you turn the heddle, you can use it as a darning frame to make sample pieces. It is also possible to produce such small articles as purses, dolls' house carpets, book markers and napkin rings.

Wind the warp directly onto the loom with one or more threads to each notch according as to how close you want the warp. Stick down the ends on the back of the loom with sellotape.

At the top and bottom of the loom, insert the small shed rods which hold the warp in position in the correct order, by passing one rod over and under alternate warp threads. Introduce the other rod in the same shed and push each rod to one end of the loom. Gather the opposite shed in a third stick and insert a fourth in the same shed. When the rods are in place tie them to the outer eye and slit of the loom as in figure 21.

Pass the shuttle, or a large, blunt needle through the resulting shed from left to right, darning in the other shed from right to left.

You will find it easiest to slip the shuttle through at an oblique angle.

Use the shuttle, or needle, to push back the threads until you have the quality of weave you want.

To maintain the right width you can tie two thin knitting needles to the two outer threads, 'weave' them into the edge and remove them when you have finished.

After inserting the shed rods you can darn in the same way on the back of the loom.

When the web is finished, before cutting it off you can dampen it and let it dry on the loom. Pressing will then not be necessary.

Belt and spectacle case

You will find it both pleasant and practical to be able to weave a belt in those colours which best match your wardrobe` and this you can do on a ribbon loom. There are many different materials which will be suitable such as cotton, wool, raffia and twine either separately or in combination with one another, and which may produce really interesting and attractive results.

Materials. The belt and spectacle case have been made of really strong, sturdy wool in various thicknesses. Measure out a suitable length of warp, that is to say a minimum of the waist measurement

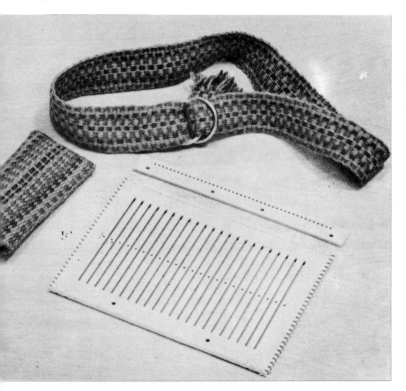

Belt and spectacle case. Both articles are woven with the same warp from yarn of various thicknesses in blues and turquoises. The clasp consists of two rings.

including the overlap and a piece for sewing on the buckle, plus about 12 to 14 inches (30–35 cm) extra for shrinkage. If you want to make a spectacle case on the same warp you will need about another 14 inches (35 cm).

Dressing the loom. Cut 45 lengths in the colours and materials you wish to use. If you want to make a symmetrical pattern start threading from the middle out to one side, then reverse the pattern out to the other side. Insert the threads alternately through slits and eyes. The easiest way to do this is by standing the heddle up and threading with a needle, as in figure 17. Stick the back ends of the threads individually through the holes on the width holder and knot them in fours. Then follow the instructions for ribbon weaving.

The belt is woven in a width of just under 2 inches (4½ cm). When you have woven the required length and want to start on the spectacle case insert a piece of paper to mark the space, remembering to allow for fringing on the end of the belt.

The spectacle case. Separate the threads till they cover a width of about 3¼ inches (8 cm) and weave till the web is 12 inches (30 cm) long. Take the work off the loom. Sew two rings onto the end of the belt and stitch along the fabric at the other end to stop it fraying when the fringes are cut.

Back the spectacle case as follows: turn the warp threads to the back of the work, tack them down and stitch along the double edge to prevent fraying.

Use card or buckram to stiffen the fabric. Cut it the same shape as the web. The lining will hold it in place when sewn round the edges. Then double the whole lot over and oversew down the sides.

Variations on ribbon weaving

Apart from weaving backwards and forwards in the ordinary way you can produce various different effects with all kinds of ribbon weaving. Here are some suggestions.

Circular weaving is achieved by always inserting the shuttle from the same side, though you must remember to change the shed between each weft thread (see figure 22). Pull the weft thread evenly and be sure to organize the pattern properly. Strips woven like this can be used for bag handles, cords, laces, etc.

Fringing. Place a small, flat stick alongside the warp on one side. An ice-lolly stick or spatula of some kind will do. Loop the weft thread round the stick and back into the same shed. Then change the shed and repeat the process (see figure 23). This kind of fringing can be used to trim such things as dresses, woollies and bags.

Cross weaving. As you can see in figure 24 the warp threads of the cross piece are made from the weft threads of the main web. Leave as many threads as you wish, of the correct length, at the side of the work while you continue on the original web. Then thread the loose end into the web, knot the ends and start weaving at the side of the finished piece.

Apart from the procedures already mentioned all kinds of ribbon looms afford endless possibilities of varying the pattern with pick-up sticks. Instructive guidance in these methods can be found in various books which you can borrow from the library.

Laces, elastic hairband, watch strap and pendant band

Here are some ideas for useful and distinctive woven strips which can be made on a ribbon loom.

It is fun to make *laces* to match your dress or coat. We have made them with eleven threads of cotton yarn. The ends have been woven in a circular weave and dipped in glue or varnish to keep a stiff point on them. This way the lace will be easier to pass through the hole. One of the laces illustrated has been woven flat, the other woven circularly half way along.

The *hairband* can be woven as an ordinary long strip or round in a piece. It is a good idea to weave a thin elastic thread in together with the wool or cotton yarn. For this you can buy shirring elastic which comes in many colours. Set the elastic on the loom with the rest of the warp, ensuring that it is stretched slightly as you dress the loom. If you wish to weave the band all in one piece you will see how to do so on the next page.

Procedure. Start by measuring round the head. Then find a box which will make a band a little larger than this measurement when the warp is threaded right round it. Stick down the end of the thread with sellotape and wind the wool and elastic together round the box until the warp reaches the width you require.

22. *Circular weaving.*
23. *Fringing.*
24. *Cross weaving.*

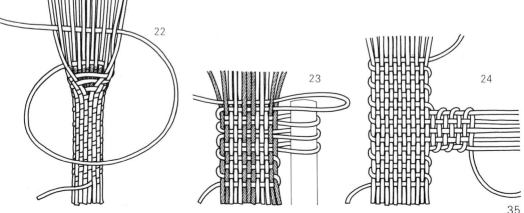

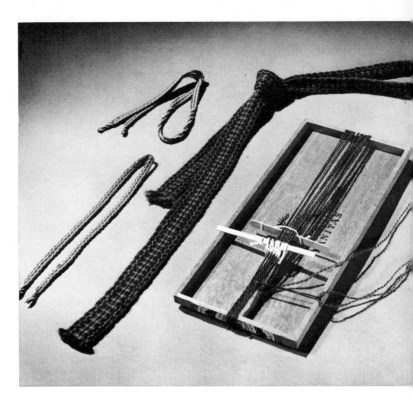

Ribbon weaving can be used for many things, for example, ties, laces, hairbands, etc. You can make these partly with rigid heddles, partly, as shewn in the picture, round the lid of a cigar box on which an elasticated hairband is being woven.

Fasten the end of the yarn with sticky tape. Insert a small pin over and under one thread plus the elastic right through the warp to make the first shed. The thread and the elastic should continue together. The other shed can be made as shown in figure 5 on page 16 with loops from a stick.

As the weaving progresses, push or pull the warp round so that it is comfortable to weave. Weave right over the ends of the warp so that they show as little as possible. Then when you have finished pull the band off the loom.

A watch strap can be made to the exact length and width you require. Buy a buckle to fasten it with. If you use a combination of different materials you will achieve an interesting effect. Try cotton, twine, and flax, for example.

A pendant band for round the neck can be woven from the materials named above. In this case you will probably want to make a very narrow ribbon for which linen thread or sewing cotton are most suitable. You can make a band like this either flat or round.

Stretcher loom

For centuries the people of many countries have woven cloth or rag rugs. Sweden and Norway are particularly noted for their fine, old tradition in this respect. The cloth, which was often coloured with vegetable dyes before being woven, was usually made of cotton or flax and cut into as long strips as possible to be wound into balls and kept until there was enough for the projected rug.

Anyone who has visited Scandinavia will doubtless have been enchanted by the extremely fine carpets, often rich in both colour and pattern, which look so well on wooden floors.

Nowadays the idea of weaving with cloth has been carried over into a great many other aspects of weaving involving different techniques, picture weaving for example. This particular technique has been used by children in recent years with interesting results. For this purpose you can, for example, use a stretcher or just some pieces of wood joined into a frame over which the warp is stretched as in figure 25. (For practical purposes it is better to stand the loom on end with the squared paper at the top.) Not only frame looms, but any of the small looms mentioned in this book, can be used for cloth weaving.

The size of the web will depend on the internal dimensions of the stretcher. You can start weaving right up by the wood at one end but will have to reckon on a space of 2-4 inches (5-10 cm) at the other end and at the sides to allow for the passage of the shuttle. (The picture overleaf shows a small rag rug woven as a test.)

25. Dressing a stretcher loom. Each loop round the frame makes two warp threads. Glue squared paper onto the frame to keep the threads evenly distributed.

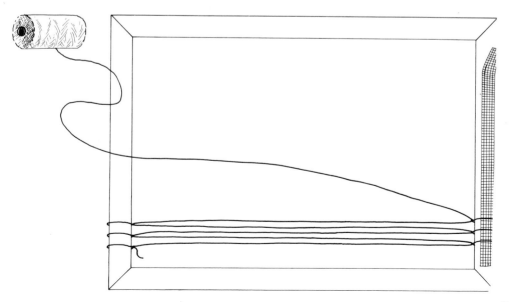

Work woven on a stretcher with rags. In this case the stretcher has been used to make a sample of cloth weaving. At the top you can see a pick-up stick used to make the first shed. On the right a small cushion woven on a stretcher loom.

Dressing a stretcher loom. To achieve an even distribution of the warp threads you can either mark the wood every 2-4 inches (5-10 cm) or glue on squared paper. Tie the warp firmly to one end of the frame pass it across to the other side and knot it round the wood, and then back across and so on (see figure 25).

For a rag rug you will need 22 warp threads for every 4 inches (10 cm). Remember that every loop round the frame means two warp threads across the loom. Use sisal for the warp. As the warp shows quite clearly in the finished web it is best to match it to the weft to a certain extent. You may, for example, dye it with Dylon.

When you have threaded the warp make a *shed* by inserting a flat stick (a shuttle, pick-up stick or something like that) alternately over and under one thread at the opposite end to where the weaving is to begin.

For the *weft* you should use rags more or less an inch wide depending on how thick the material is. If you are using fairly stout or stiff fabric it is best to cut it on the cross. Sew the strips together into a long 'cord' or cut them diagonally across the ends and let them overlap a little when joining them as you weave. Do the same thing when changing colours.

It is usually best to weave a few rows with the warp thread before starting with the rags.

Weave as follows: introduce the weft alternately over and under one thread, going over and under the opposite threads on the next row. Unlike an ordinary loom, this kind makes it impossible to create two sheds by alternately raising and lowering half the threads, so you will have to gather up every other shed with a stick sawn diagonally across one end. Make the other shed by lifting the flat stick which is inserted in the warp. At the top of the picture on page 38 you can see a stick of this kind, called a pattern stick. A stick of this kind is used to gather up the warp threads.

Keep the weave close with a strong tapestry beater.

When the web is finished, cut the threads at the ends of the frame.

You can also take the stretcher to pieces and draw off the web. Knot the warp threads to secure the ends of the web.

Poncho — woven on a stretcher loom

You don't need a large and expensive loom to produce this poncho, but you do need a lot of patience and a certain degree of accuracy. You can achieve excellent results if you choose colours and materials that go well with each other and are well-suited to the purpose.

We thought it right to include the poncho in this book although it is a bit more difficult to make because it is impossible to produce anything similar on a conventional loom.

The same kind of loom, but in smaller dimensions, can be used to weave such articles as scarves.

Materials. Use really strong, coarse wool yarn in orange, yellow and brown colours. The yarn is taken double for both warp and weft.

Making the loom. Shops dealing in artists' materials stock stretcher pieces of any length which can be fitted together to make any size. When you have finished weaving you can dismantle them and use them again later in other combinations. They are what painters use to stretch their canvas. You can also make frames from pieces of wood firmly joined at right angles in the corners. You will also need four flat pick-up sticks or shuttles and a long flat pattern stick sawn off in a diagonal at one end. The stretcher used here measures 40 inches square. Push the corners together and make sure that the corners are at exact right angles, in a door frame for example. Mark the centre point on all four sides and continue marking the wood out towards the corners at a distance of 4 inches on each side.

Poncho. This warm and colourful poncho is woven on a large stretcher. It is work for more advanced weavers and requires a great deal of patience to produce the finished article. But then the result will be unlike anything you could make on a 'real' loom. It is woven in yellow, orange and brown.

26. See right. How to start dressing the loom for the poncho. Then build out gradually on all four sides.

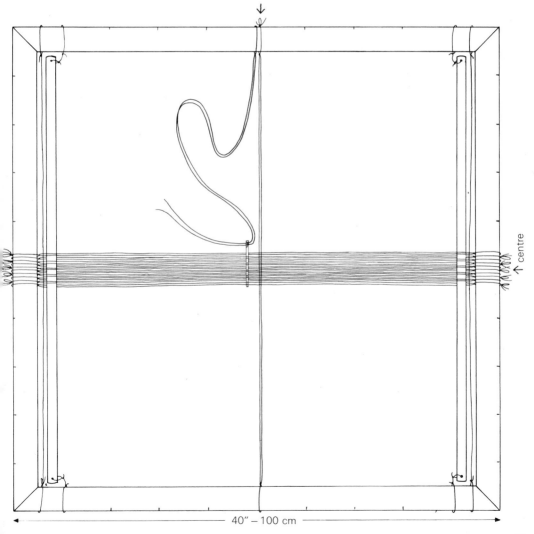

centre →

←———— 40″ – 100 cm ————→

41

Dressing the loom. Cut the warp thread into pieces about 86 inches long. It is best to start by cutting just a few pieces and checking that they are the right length. Work with two threads tied on together throughout. Position the loom in a convenient place. You can rest the bottom edge on the floor and the top against a wall or some such sturdy object. Be careful not to let the centre section come into contact with anything or it may easily be stretched. You shouldn't fix the frame as you will have to turn it the whole time.

Weaving (or darning). Tie ten double threads to two opposite sides of the frame as follows: double the thread and loop it over the frame tying it with a single knot. Pass the two threads over to the opposite side and make another single knot before fastening the ends in a tight bow around the wood. As the bows take up quite a lot of room it is advisable to place them alternately at one end then the other. When fastened on the ten double threads should take up just over 5 inches (13 cm) of the frame and amount to 40 threads altogether. This means that the closeness of the weave is about 30-34 threads to 4 inches (10 cm).

Darn in the first weft threads at right angles as shewn in figure 26. To keep the threads in the right order, insert a cord at the outer edge, alternately over and under one thread with a pick-up stick, a shuttle or a flat piece of wood taking up the opposite threads as in figure 26. When placed on its edge this will make the first shed while the other is produced by a pattern stick, a flat piece of wood cut diagonally across one end.

Insert this through the opposite threads to the previous shed, lift it on its edge and you have made another shed. It is best to turn the frame round so that you are always weaving from top to bottom and bottom to top. You will find that when the weft is threaded onto a really heavy, long upholstery needle it will slip quite easily through the shed because raising the pick-up stick and the pattern stick respectively makes an extremely good shed.

It is best to proceed by weaving in six to eight double threads, pulling them tight and tying them to the other side of the frame

27. Use cross weaving for the yoke as this will make the cut for the neck opening more secure, and for the borders.

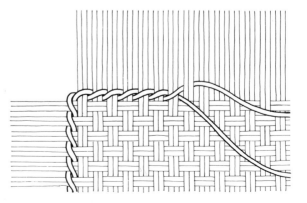

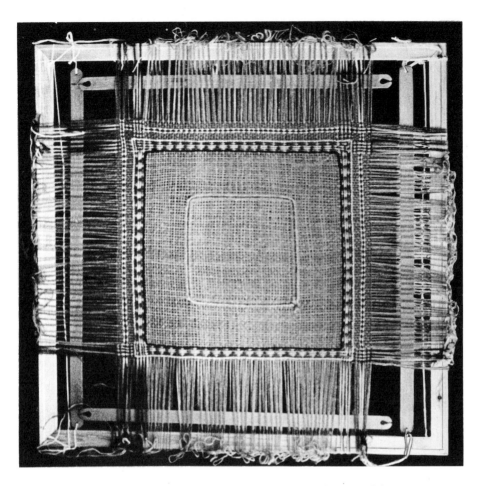

before turning the whole loom. As you work insert a pick-up stick (and even at the outer edge a piece of string) to retain the correct thread order and to ensure that as further threads are introduced they are correctly positioned along the stick. Then you will be able to make a shed with the stick.

As you continue weaving, turn the loom so that it is still in the most comfortable position. Build the web outwards on all four sides working about six double threads before each turn. Press down the threads with a beater, a large comb or similar tool.

When the web measures about 10 inches (25 cm), after about 38 double threads in each direction, cross weave for three to four rows with matching yarn, using either single or double, on all four sides. One of the reasons for this is to make a firm border to keep the threads in place and at the same time to make a yoke. The neck opening will later be made within this edging (see figure 27 and the picture on page 40).

Stretcher loom on which a poncho is being woven. The pins and shuttles are used to make one shed, the other is gathered up with a long pattern stick which is raised to insert the weft.

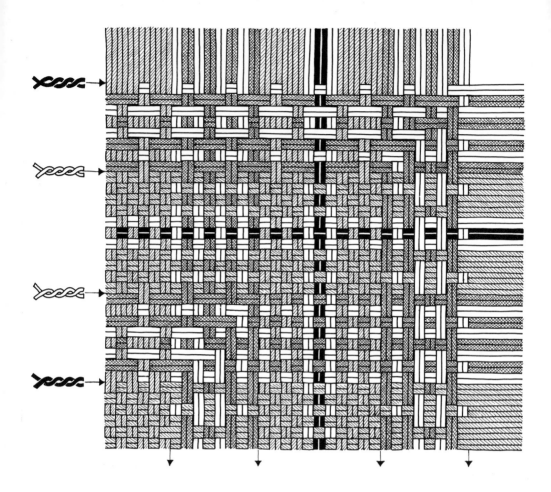

*28. Diagrammatic
representation of the
border.*

Then continue with ordinary weaving as before on all four sides for 4-5 inches (10-12 cm). Follow this with a row of cross weaving before making the patterned border in appropriate colours, as in figure 28. Note that the pattern is made by weaving over and under the threads indicated in the diagram and following this by weaving another colour over and under the opposite threads to make the pattern stand out.

If the web seems to be getting slightly loose in places, rows of cross weaving on each side of the border pattern will hold the threads firm.

When the web measures about 28 inches (70 cm), finish it off by cross weaving. You can make the web larger, but in that case you should remove the flat pin before continuing.

44

Before removing the web from the stretcher, dampen it thoroughly with a sponge and tease it all over with a stiff nail brush, brushing diagonally across the work, until the surface achieves the desired 'shaggy' effect.

Untie the *knots* or bows and remove the web. Cut the fringe to the required length.

Make a line of tacking stitches from one corner of the inner square to the other and machine stitch closely along this line several times to fasten the web; use zig-zagging if you can. Place a strip of material about 1½ inches (4 cm) wide along the lines of stitching, right sides together and machine stitch it on (see figure 29).

Cut the slit carefully open, turn the facing through to the wrong side and hem it firmly to the back of the work.

29. Neck opening.
1) Stop the fabric from fraying by sewing small machine stitches along a tacking thread.
2) Attach the facing on the right side and cut the slit open.
3) Turn the facing to the wrong side and sew it down.

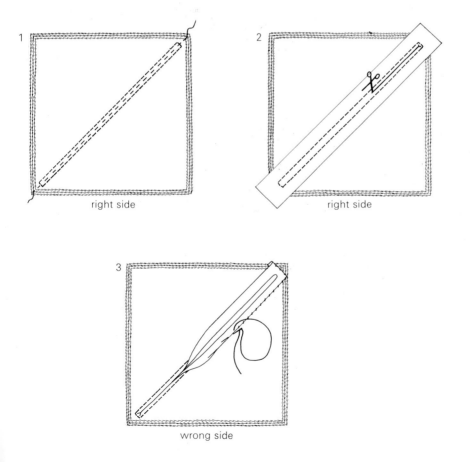

1 right side

2 right side

3 wrong side

Weaving a picture on a stretcher loom

The girl with balloons is meant to be made jointly by a group of children, since each balloon can be made separately on a little disc of cardboard (see figure 30). Use gay colours for the balloons. The actual background can be woven on a stretcher as here or may consist of a piece of material to which the girl, the sun and the balloons are fixed.

You could use the same method, getting children to make round shapes, to create a flower picture with the individual flowers in bright colours. It is also possible to make other shapes than just circular ones by weaving in this way for example houses, bushes, and trees.

Method. As you can see from the picture we have used a stretcher measuring 15 by 18 inches (38 by 46 cm). Dress the loom with linen thread, using about 50 threads to every 4 inches (10 cm) which will mean 90 threads altogether spread over the 7 inches (18 cm) or so which is the width of the web (see figure 25 on page 37).

You will find it easiest to do the weaving at the top and bottom if you introduce a pick-up stick. Lifting this will give you one shed while the other is made by gathering up threads on a long needle. The woven borders at top and bottom are intended to provide a casing through which a stick can be inserted to hang the picture up.

Between the borders, you can thread some thin yarn in a fairly random fashion both horizontally and diagonally, which is partly to secure the warp threads right out to the edge and partly to create a representative background for the girl.

Draw a rough sketch of the design so that you can work out how big the girl should be. It is easiest to draw a backview, with a parting down the middle of the head between two pigtails. You can either weave her directly into the warp or make her on a small cardboard shape notched at the edge to take the warp. Push the weft thread back to make the bottom of the skirt curved.

Make the hair directly onto the warp by darning it in and letting the ends stick out at the sides. Plait the ends and tie them with a bow before cutting them off. If the parting doesn't show clearly enough you can draw a light coloured thread over it.

30. Cardboard disc used for weaving the balloons. There should be an odd number of notches round the edge, the number to be determined by the thickness of the yarn.

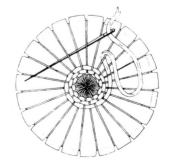

The picture can be hung up as here on the actual frame, but it has been made in such a way that it can be removed and mounted. For this you could use a bamboo cane at top and bottom. Then hang it as a decoration on the wall or in a window.

Weave the balloons by darning round suitably sized discs of cardboard (see figure 30). Do not darn right out to the edge but when you have eased the work from the disc pass the thread through all the warp ends and draw them tight. They can then be fastened to the background when you have decided where they are to go. It is best to make all the loose pieces, including the sun, before attaching them.

The sun is also made on a circular disc of cardboard. To make the 'rays' you should start a little way out from the centre and work back over one warp thread, forward under two, back over one and so on.

Vary the yellow colours slightly. On the last round insert the needle through the warp threads to prevent the weft from slipping off. Cut the warp threads in the centre of the loops, tack the whole circle firmly to the background and pass a thread from the balloons down to the girl.

Weaving frame with heddles

You can make this loom quickly and easily and use it to make many different things including bags, cushions, napkins, and scarves.

The frame consists of four pieces of wood joined at the corners with screws and wing nuts. This form of construction means that you can quite easily make looms of varying widths by joining different lengths of wood.

It is equally easy to remove the heddles, which are made on the actual frame, and arrange them on a narrower or wider loom as you wish.

It is preferable not to use too 'fluffy' a yarn for the warp as this makes it difficult to change sheds. You will find twine, cotton or for that matter any yarn which seems smooth, ideal for this purpose.

Making the frame. The frame in the photograph has been made from four pieces of wood each 13 inches (32 cm) long. If you want a wider loom make the horizontal sides longer. You will need four screws and nuts and two small headless nails to knot the heddles on.

Drill holes for the screws in all four sides, to prevent the wood from splitting.

Drill another two holes about a third of the way along the bottom of the frame. These are for sticking rods through while setting up the loom (see figure 17, page 30).

Join the corners making sure that they are all true right angles. Bang in the nails in the middle of the lefthand long side about an inch apart (see figure 31).

Heddles. Knot the heddles in twine cut into lengths of about 32 inches (80 cm). Loop the twine over the top of the frame, tie a double knot just above the top nail and one just below the bottom nail. Push the heddle along the frame and fasten it to the bottom of the frame with another double knot (see diagram). Remember that you need half as many heddles as there are warp threads.

Dressing the loom. Make the warp as shewn in figure 11, passing the thread backwards and forwards between two rounded shed rods at each end.

Fix the frame upright in a vice or a pair of crossed sticks and pass the warp threads alternately through the eyes and slits of the heddles.

Thus the frame performs the same function as the ribbon loom on page 29 as it is raised and lowered.

Proceed in the same way as for the ribbon loom. You can tie an extra thread round the shed rods or whatever sticks have been inserted behind the loom. This will correspond to the back beam on a frame loom. The warp is kept tight and even while it is rolled up and is then clamped to a table.

Roll the woven work onto the sticks holding the warp in front of the frame (see figures 31 and 32 on page 50) which correspond to the front beam on a frame loom.

Here you can see how
the heddle frame is
lifted to make a shed
through which to pass
the shuttle. The next
shed is made by
dropping the frame.

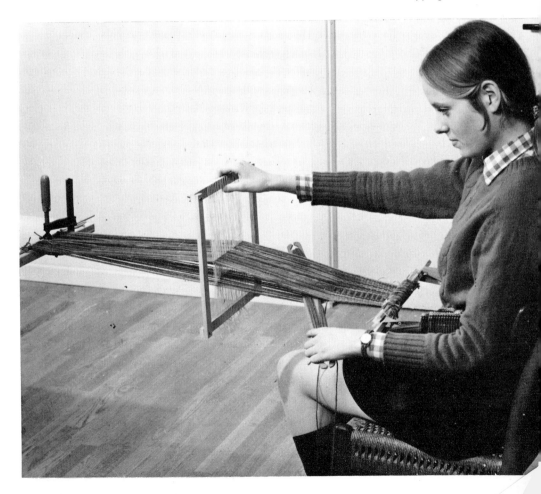

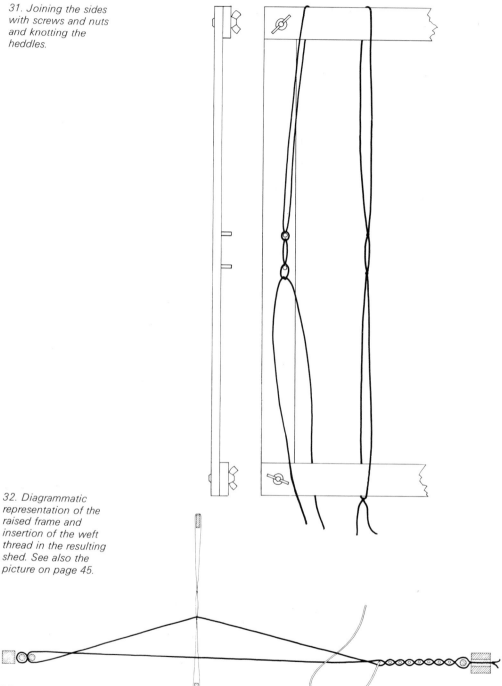

31. Joining the sides
with screws and nuts
and knotting the
heddles.

32. Diagrammatic
representation of the
raised frame and
insertion of the weft
thread in the resulting
shed. See also the
picture on page 45.

MAKING STRING THINGS

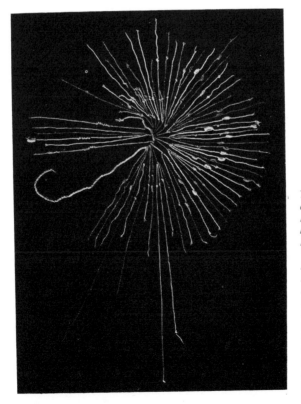

This decorative cluster
of string originated in
Peru. It is not, however,
intended as a decoration
but as a so-called
'quipu' or counting
instrument. The ancient
Indians had no written
language and relied for
the reckoning of such
things as the numbers of
llamas on knots. The
thickness of the knots
and whereabouts on the
string signify numbers
reckoned according to
the decimal system.

A few words about the materials

The examples in this section of the book have been made with *sisal* of various thicknesses, single ply or several fibres plied together. Sisal is white but goes yellow when exposed to the light.

This material is easy to work with and can be bought comparatively cheaply in many shops.

Sisal comes from the plant Agave sisalana which originated in Central America, though the bulk of sisal we import comes from Africa and Java.

The fleshy leaves are transformed into hard fibres which are stiff like horse hair and which give the twine and anything made with it a slightly bristly quality.

Sisal takes dyes well and is easy to glue together into coils and other shapes to set on a background.

Jute comes from the tall plant Corchorus. It is cheap and much used for materials such as hessian and sack cloth. It is also used for rope and binder twine and coated with tar for marine and agricultural purposes. It lacks the stiffness of sisal but its very softness makes it suitable for work in which sisal would be too firm. Jute can be used, for example, to crochet and knit with and for knotting. In many cases its brownish colour can be combined to great effect with the white of sisal or cotton twine, as in the decoration of glass found on pages 55 to 57.

Jute is obtainable in various thicknesses and can be bought ready coloured; you can also dye it yourself.

Hemp has soft fibres like jute, but is thinner and lighter in colour. It comes from the plant Cannabis sativa, a member of the hop family. The fibres are greyish or yellowish in colour and these shades can be used to make many things, including table mats and baskets.

Cotton twine is available in various forms and can be used to make any number of things. The fibres are soft and come from the seed boll or capsule of the cotton plant.

Different thicknesses of fishing yarn have been used for some of the models in the book. You may be able to buy this white or coloured, though the thicker yarns are usually white. However, since it takes dyes well enough you should be able to have whatever colour in whatever thickness you want. (See the next section on dyeing.)

Paper string can also be used to great effect in much of the work and will take dyes extremely well.

Some places also sell other materials, twine made out of palm leaves for example which looks lovely when woven into finely patterned baskets.

There are many other natural products which are suitable for the models in the book and if you can possibly get hold of them it would be a good idea to go ahead and use them.

Dyeing cord and twine

You will find it great fun and not very difficult to colour your own yarns. With a little practice it is possible to hit on exactly the shade you want, which means that you will be able to work with many different shades for a modest outlay. Using plant or vegetable dyes will give you the best and most attractive results though bought dyes are easier to work with and achieve good results.

Well suited to our purpose are the powder and liquid dyes sold in the shops for furnishings and so on. You will also need an old saucepan and a couple of bowls. You can use newspaper and polythene to cover the surrounding area and to lay the materials on when they have been dyed and rinsed. You should follow the instructions for 'hot water dyes'.

It is a good idea to work with two different dyes at once as you can make a great number of between shades in this way. You can also vary the colours by using a strong or weak solution of the dye. If you choose a yellow and a blue dye, for example, you will be able to achieve a whole range of greens as well as the original colours. Combining red with yellow will create endless red, gold and orange shades while adding red to blue will give various purple and violets.

It can be a lot of fun to dye even really small pieces of twine. You can use them for the fishes on page 84, which have actually been made of little bits of string dipped in different dye baths so that the colours have run slightly into each other. You could make an enjoyable game out of it.

Before putting the twine in the dye bath you should untie any knots and carry out a sample dyeing. Put the twine in the dye bath and move it around with an implement like an old fork. Then lift it out with the fork and immerse it in a bowl of cold water. Rinse it till no more dye will come out, then give it one more rinse with a little vinegar in the water. Hang the twine up to dry or lay it on the newspaper, turning it now and again as it dries.

Sisal twine is inclined to unravel when wet, so it pays to fasten the ends before you start dyeing.

Glue, varnish and a few hints

The *glue* used in most of the models is synthetic resin glue which dries to a transparent finish. It dries very quickly, which is handy since you can see the end result very soon.

If the glue becomes too thick while you are working with it you can thin it with a little water but this will make it less adhesive. Remember always to replace the top when you're not using it.

Varnishing. It is practical to protect the string against wet and dirt.

You may also want the finished article to be more stiff. So the answer is to varnish it.

You can do this with cellulose varnish and a thinning liquid. Mix half and half, and apply to the article with a soft brush.

If you want a stronger finish you can varnish the work several times but you should let each coat dry before applying the next.

Cellulose varnish is inflammable and has a very strong smell. So you should not use it anywhere near a naked flame and take care to air the room well afterwards.

You can use other kinds of varnish, but in that case it is best to consult your paint merchant.

A few hints about workmanship. As many of the yarns used in this book tend to unravel at the ends it is useful to secure these with a little blob of glue. When you have applied the glue you can roll the ends into a thin point like a shoe lace.

This will help, for example, when you wish to weave with the twine as you can use the end like a kind of needle. This sort of work often makes it impossible to use even a very big needle, but following the above advice you should seldom feel the need to do so.

You can also use glue when joining or piecing twine. You should unravel the two ends to be joined and possibly thin them out slightly. Then spread a little glue on them and roll them together so that the join is virtually the same thickness as the actual twine. You should reckon on the join being stiffer than the rest of the twine.

When starting or ending a piece of binding work you should thin the ends a little before glueing them on the covered surface, though this doesn't apply to such cases as double coils.

Winding coils

It is easy enough to wind coils — easy enough for the children too — and they can be used to decorate in many ways. See the diagram on page 57.

The main point to remember is to start from the centre. Moisten the end of the string with a synthetic resin glue and twist it into a coil dabbing a little glue onto the edge of the twine before winding on the next circle. In this way you can ensure that the whole coil is joined by glue all the way round.

If you just want the one coil you should thin out the end of the string to make the fastening off point as flat as possible. You can clip or pin the glued end in place while it is drying.

When making a double coil, start by winding one without any glue to work out how much string it takes. Then crease the string over.

Start winding the string as already described until you reach the crease. Hold the part you have glued fast with a paper clip or a pin and start coiling from the other end. Finally, make sure that the coils are the same size.

When you have made the coils, spread glue on the back and press them firmly onto the article you wish to decorate until dry. If necessary you can leave them under a heavy object.

If the sisal twine looks too 'hairy' you can trim it before and after use with a pair of scissors.

You can also try singeing off the small hairs over a gas flame or a spirit flame, but this must be done very carefully as white sisal can all too easily be scorched.

1. Binding a vase.

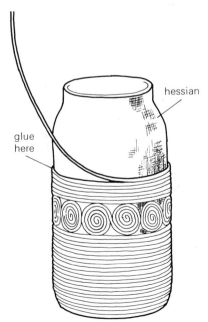

hessian

glue here

Decorative coil work

Recent years have seen the production of a great many bottles and glasses in attractive and interesting shapes, many of them admirably suited for decoration. More conventional glassware also provides a good foundation for work of this kind; see, for example, the instant coffee jar in the photograph.

A jam jar and an instant coffee jar provide excellent bases for binding with twine or string, either in the natural colours available in these materials or with dyed twine.

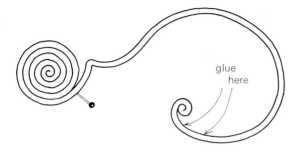

glue
here

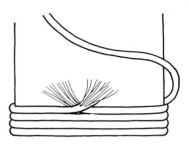

Procedure. After cleaning all paper and labels off the glass attach a piece of soft, thin hessian using a synthetic resin glue, making sure that it fits exactly at top and bottom (see figure 1).

You can use a thick jute yarn in a brownish colour for the binding. Start at the bottom of the jar, glueing the first layer carefully on round the edge. Then, when the glue has dried, continue binding until just before half way up. Cut the twine diagonally across and glue the end down neatly.

The coils. Measure round the jar. The large jar is about 12 inches (30 cm) round, and has been decorated with six double coils which means that they have to be about 2 inches (5 cm) per pair. The coils are made in really soft, white, cotton string. It is best to make a test coil first to measure how much string it takes. Then cut off double that amount. The actual coiling is done in the following way: crease the piece of string half way along and start twisting from one end, glueing as you go. Continue this till you reach the crease as in the diagram. Hold the first coil with a clip or pin and now wind the second coil in the same way (see figure 2).

Make sure that they are the right size. When all the coils are finished, glue them on the hessian backing and continue binding with jute yarn up to the top of the jar. Glue it evenly onto the hessian taking especial care where the jar curves in. Stick the end in under the last round at the top and glue it neatly in place.

Finally, varnish the jar to make the binding less fragile.

Binding glass

You can bind instant coffee or jam jars with different coloured string of various qualities by winding it directly onto the glass. You should let the first round at the bottom dry before carrying on with the binding.

Join ends of string by unravelling the ends and covering them with the next round which is glued down (see figure 3).

If very rough sisal or some other fibrous twine is being used you can trim or singe it before varnishing if you wish.

2. Procedure for double coils.

3. Piecing the binding twine on jars and vases.

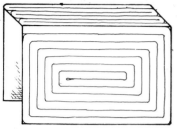

4. For a matchbox cover, start winding round the edges of the surface and continue inwards.

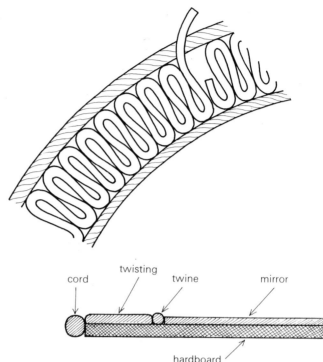

5. Twisting the pattern.

6. Cross section of the edge.

cord   twisting   twine   mirror

hardboard

Decorating boxes

A zinc cover has been made for three sides of the matchbox in the photograph so that you can easily change the box or turn it round when the striking side has been used up. See the photograph on page 56.

In this case we have decorated the top with coils of different coloured sisal twine in reddy orange shades and the side and bottom with red cotton twine. Venetian blind string provides an excellent material since it is easy to coil into the required shapes and takes dye well.

It is safest to start from the outside and work inwards or you may have problems making the coiling fit (see figure 4).

This technique can be used for many kinds of decorations, bookbinding, for example, and file covers.

Larger decorations of twisted twine

Both circular and rectangular mirrors are suitable for decoration in cord or sisal twine of various thicknesses, though this form of ornamentation can also be adapted for many other purposes, using strong or thin twine.

In this case we shall explain how to decorate a mirror.

Natural and dyed sisal have been used to decorate the bottle. It is easiest to make the twisted edge round the mirror with a soft cord, like cotton blind cord.

Procedure. You can either use the backing board as it is or, as here, give it a coat of acrylic paint round the edge before glueing on the mirror glass.

Spread an even layer of synthetic resin glue on the back of the mirror and stick it in position. It will help to mark the exact place beforehand. Lay a couple of books on top to hold the mirror in place until it is dry.

Then glue a length of cord around the edge of the mirror. This should preferably be of the same thickness as the mirror so that it hides the edge. Cut the two ends straight across and apply a little glue so that the ends fit exactly together. You should use a synthetic resin glue in this case also as it dries to a transparent finish. Hold the join in place with clips or sellotape until dry.

Start sticking on the pattern in the same way, preferably where the twine is running straight as it will be difficult to make the final join on a curve (see figure 5). The best material to use is twine which is not too stiff like cotton blind cord and which can be dyed if you wish. At the outer edge we have used a piece of sisal clothesline coloured a little darker than the inner twine and the backing board.

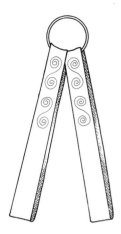

7. Tray hanger.

The outer ring of cord should be thick enough to cover both the backing board and the twisted twine. Stick it round the edge, joining the ends as described above. Figure 6 provides a summary of the various stages.

To hang the mirror up you should cut a suitable length of cord, unravel the ends and glue them firmly to the back in such a way that the hanging cord is invisible (see diagram 22 on page 72).

Binding a bottle with a clothes-line

Bottles of various shapes, sizes and colours can be bound with natural or coloured twine or cord. This also applies to any other kind of cylindrical container.

We have used a bottle with a heavy, protruding layer of glass at the bottom. You should glue the first row of twine just above this layer and leave it to dry.

The handle and the pairs of decorative, unravelled strings have been made of coloured sisal clothes-line in two shades.

Measure out the required length of coloured cord, in this case twice 27 inches (68 cm) for the handles and four times $3\frac{1}{2}$ inches (9 cm) for the tassels. Unravel the ends a little and glue them firmly to the bottle just above the first round of binding at regular intervals.

Continue binding for several rounds covering the handles and tassels and then going over and under as the pattern demands; see also page 64. If you spread a little glue on the bottle under the cord you can be sure it is secure. You should also glue the last round particularly carefully. You can disguise the fastening off point best if you taper the twine and secure it under one of the tassels.

Making coils on webbing

For things like tray hangers you can use both webbing and the kind of tape used for edging carpets. Both are of a suitable width. We have used coils to decorate our model (figure 7) but there is ample room for imaginative thinking here. Make the coils in your hand before sticking them on the tape. Loop the bands round a ring and sew them together. See also page 67 on working with webbing. You can use the same idea for belts.

Winding table mats

The table mat shewn opposite has been made of ordinary, old-fashioned clothes-line, coiled and glued together. The finished article measures about 6–7 inches (16 cm) across. As you can see from figure 8 it consists of three double and one single coils. Each of the double coils takes about 36 inches (85 cm) and the single half as much. It is a good idea to roll a loose coil beforehand to measure how much cord it takes. See the explanation on page 57.

When you have finished twisting the coils you can lay them together as shewn and join them with a strong thread by sewing alternately into first one, then another coil at the point of contact.

The tray hanger and knitting needle holder are ideal for anyone who wishes to make something useful which doesn't take too long. The table mat is composed of rigid coils of sisal cord.

You can apply a little glue as you press them together to make the join extra secure.

Then glue a double row of cord all the way round taking care to fasten the ends well with glue, and possibly thinning them out slightly to make the break as unnoticeable as possible.

If the mat is inclined to bulge in odd places you can dampen it slightly with a sponge and put it in a press. Then, when dry, it can be varnished and made heatproof should you so wish.

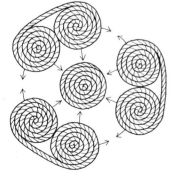

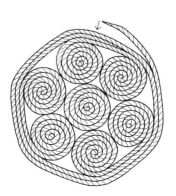

8. Join the double coils round the single one, then sew and glue two rows of cord round the edge.

Fabulous animals made of string

To decorate the box coils of string have been twisted in random fashion, some of them heaped up like imaginery snail shells.

You may sometimes be lucky enough to acquire a cigar box with a hinged lid and even a catch of some kind, but failing this, any kind of box will do.

Cut a piece of cardboard to fit the lid and cover it. We have used turquoise coloured hessian for this purpose. Fold the edges of the fabric to the back of the cardboard and glue them down. Then glue the whole lot onto the lid and let it dry under pressure.

Glue a piece of string in a darker shade round the edge. The animals are coiled and glued together from various different materials in turquoise and yellowy green. There is ample opportunity to use your imagination here.

Binding

Paperknife

Most paint shops sell flat, spatula-shaped sticks which are used to stir paint with. But they can also be turned to many other uses. In this case we have transformed just such a stick into a paperknife. Make a point on the stick with a fretsaw or a knife, file it evenly out to make a sharp edge and finally sandpaper it smooth.

If you are intending to bind the handle in a dark colour it is best to paint the light-coloured wood with watercolour in the same shade so that it doesn't show through.

Cut the threads which go to form the pattern double the length of the area to be bound. Glue them firmly to the end of knife in the order you have envisaged, holding them in place with sticky tape until the glue has dried (see figure 9).

Fasten the yarn to be used for binding under the pattern threads with a little glue.

The paperknife in the photograph has been bound with fishing yarn which can be bought in various colours. The seven threads which go to form the pattern are placed on the handle with a space about the thickness of the yarn between them (see figure 10). If these threads are too close together you won't be able to bind the pattern properly.

9. Glue the pattern threads onto the paperknife.

glue here

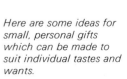

Here are some ideas for small, personal gifts which can be made to suit individual tastes and wants.

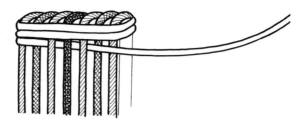

10. How to start binding the pattern.

Make the fastening-off as invisible as possible by sticking the end under the last round and glueing it down.

This kind of work affords opportunities for working out your own patterns or for using cross-stitch or weaving patterns. You could use the same method to weave in initials, following a cross-stitch pattern.

You can protect the decoration with varnish if you wish.

Bangle

You can decorate a bangle according to the same principle as the paperknife. The advantage of this kind of work is that it is so cheap that you could make several at a time in different colours. Space the pattern threads slightly apart and glue on the ends. Then, as you wind, bend those threads which create the pattern back when the binding thread passes underneath them and forward again to be replaced by others as the pattern demands (see figure 11).

You can either buy a wooden bangle to form the basis of your work or, as here, make do with a ring of cardboard. Indeed, many materials can be used provided you make sure that the synthetic resin glue will adhere to the surface concerned.

Before starting to bind you should mark off divisions the size of one pattern repeat on the bangle to be certain that the pattern will fit all the way round. Obviously the smaller the pattern the easier it will be to adjust but you should bind a test piece first.

11. How to bind the pattern in.

We have also used fishing yarn for the bangle, but you could try

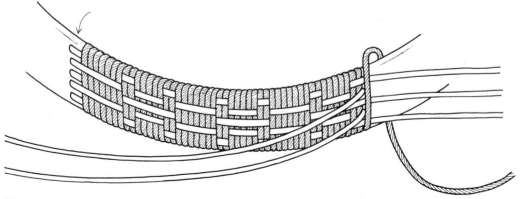

other kinds of twine as long as they don't scratch the skin.

Varnish the bangle when you have finished.

Pattern binding

You can make this beaker, which can be used for cigarettes, as a pencil holder or for anything you wish, from a thick cardboard roll cut over at a suitable length. The bottom can be sealed with a piece of thick card.

Draw a circle round the inside, as shewn in figure 12. Cut this out, spread glue round the edge and press it up inside to form a base. To make the bottom firmer you can cut another piece of strong paper a little larger than the base. Cut notches round the edge of it, fold them up round the beaker and glue firmly.

Paint the beaker with plastic paint.

You can use jute, sisal or cotton twine to bind with. Glue down the whole of the first round of binding then unravel the ends of the pattern threads and glue them on at regular intervals. When the glue is dry continue binding upwards, over and under the pattern threads. You can make the beaker more resistant to damage if you varnish it.

Binding rolls of cardboard

The case in the photograph on page 61 is designed for knitting needles. It is made of two cardboard rolls, one of which fits inside the other. The pipe with the smaller diameter should be fairly long while the lid is made from the wider pipe. The bottom on both case and lid is made as in figure 12.

Bind the lid in sisal twine starting with the centre of the coil. Moisten the end of the twine with glue and twist it round closely. Use the glue every time you wind a new round. Coil the twine in

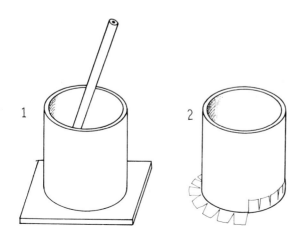

*12. Fit the bottom of
the beaker with
cardboard and paper.*

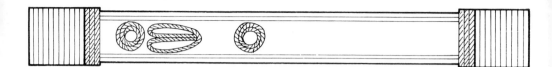

14. The decorated
knitting needle case.

your hand until you have the required size and glue it on to fit the
flat surface of the lid. Continue binding closely down the sides of
the lid to the bottom edge. Cut the twine diagonally across and
glue the end down (see figure 13). You can hold the end down
with a paper clip until the glue has dried completely.

Make the bottom of the case in the same way, binding the same
length up the sides as the depth of the lid, unless you prefer to
bind the whole thing.

Give the cardboard one coat of paint on the outside, and the lid
a coat on the inside. Paint the edges before you start binding.

Glue four pieces of soft twine the length of the case as decoration,
covering the ends with more twine wound round.

You can use whatever form of decoration you wish. In this case,
we have made a little coiled flower with a centre gap. The leaves
are made by glueing both ends of a piece of twine so that they lie
parallel for a little way, and then turning the loop back and under
the ends to make a base (see figure 13). The end result can be
seen in figure 14.

Decorations on webbing

The webbing you can buy at a saddlers or in a carpet shop is the
right width for making a spectacle case which will not need much
stiffening.

It takes about two feet of webbing, with thin, white cotton
twine used for the decoration.

The straight lines of the pattern are made in brown jute twine.

Divide the webbing into four pieces of equal sizes with a tacking
thread. One or both the inner quarters can be decorated. Start by
drawing the brown twine through the webbing at intervals of four
or five threads (see figure 15).

13. Decorating the
knitting needle case.

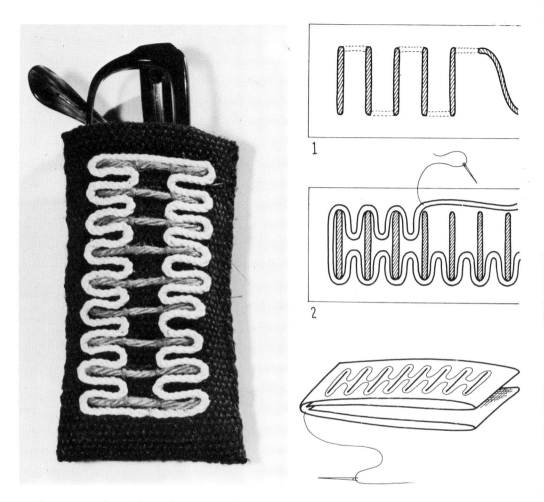

Then curve the white twine round the brown, catching it down with small stitches at each fold. Dab a little glue on the ends before joining them with invisible stitching.

Mounting the webbing. Double over the two outer quarters and adjust the ends so that they just reach the bottom inside.

Sew the case down the sides. You can use a little thread unravelled from the webbing for this if you wish (see figure 16).

If you want the case stiffened, insert a piece of cardboard between the two layers of webbing on one side.

For the use of webbing see also pages 60 and 61.

15. Decorating the webbing (1 and 2).

16. Sewing the case.

You can make these table mats, as here, with oddments of packing twine, or with coloured string.

Working on a weaving ring

Circular weaving

A weaving ring can be used to make many things of different kinds and is both fun and easy to work with. It is an especially good loom to work with if you have poor sight.

We start by describing the traditional way you can use the ring for such articles as table mats, and go on to detail other methods.

In this case the ring is about 9 inches (22 cm) across and has twenty-five holes.

Before starting work you should number the holes to make dressing the warp easier (see figures 17 and 18).

Table mats

The mats in the picture have been made of fishing yarn, sisal and jute yarn. You will get the best results from using the same kind of yarn for the warp and the outer rows of weaving.

Dress the loom with one long thread.

Tie this to hole number 1, pass it over the edge to hole 14 and through this from the outside. Then go across the inner side of the ring to hole 15 and out through there. If you are making a small mat, a coaster or something like that, you can dress the warp as in figure 18.

Follow the sequence
from hole 15 to hole 2
from hole   3 to hole 16
from hole 17 to hole 4.

Continue in this way until there is only hole 13 left (see figure 18). Then take the thread over the centre point and down between holes 1 and 25, and up again between 13 and 12 as in the diagram. In this way you can fasten the centre point and make sure that it lies exactly in the middle. Start weaving with the rest of the warp thread by interlacing over thread number 12, under number 11, over 10 and so on.

17. Dressing the warp for table mats.

18. Weaving ring prepared for a small article (see also page 73)

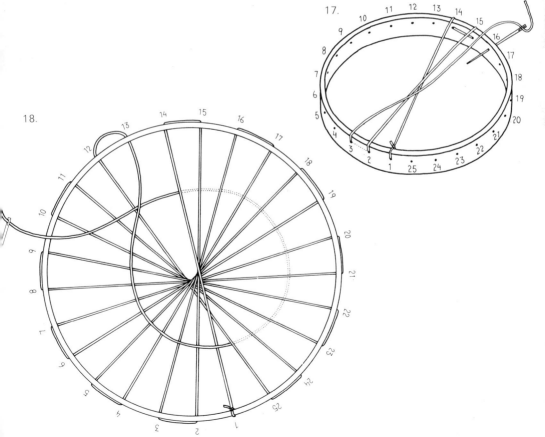

If the warp thread is fairly thick, the middle will stick up, though you can make it a bit flatter by pressing with a damp cloth afterwards.

You can change to a new thread by letting the two ends run side by side for a while, making sure that the loose ends lie at the back of the work where you can trim them off later.

You can use oddments of packing twine to weave with. If you can find different shades the results will be excellent. Otherwise coloured string will do just as well.

Should you wish to make patterns, then you are not just confined to the stripes produced by changing the colour of the thread row by row. Instead you can weave over one thread in one colour and over the next in another alternately, or cross weave as in figure 19. In both these cases there will come a point in the row where you will have to go over two warp threads as this kind of rayed pattern requires an even number of warp threads.

When the mat measures about 6 inches (16 cm), cut the threads inside the ring and darn the ends down alongside the next thread in the row (see figure 20). For larger mats see page 72.

You can press the mat under a damp cloth and varnish it.

Flower picture made on a weaving ring

Following the technique already described you can make different round-headed flowers. The sunflower has been woven on a ring, but instead of sewing in the warp ends they have been unravelled and left. Stop the edges from coming undone by putting a thin line of glue round the outside, but make sure that you don't get any glue on the threads you are going to unravel.

You can use sisal for the flower, dyeing it orange, yellow and red for the purpose. The bristly quality of the twine gives the centre of the flower a rough look admirably suited to the motif.

Extra threads in matching colours have been inserted round the outside of the flower to create more fullness round the edge.

19. Cross weaving with two threads.

20. Finish at the edge with a row of cross weaving, then thread the warp threads down alongside the next thread.

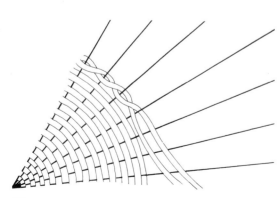

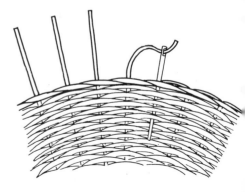

This sun flower picture (actual size 20 by 36 inches) has been partly made on a weaving ring and partly formed in the hand. The picture is in warm, golden tones — orangy colours for the flowers and yellowy greens for stalk and leaves.

21. How to wind the leaves.

The actual weaving should be carried out as described above except that the outer rows should be pulled tight so that when the work is cut off the ring it will curve out slightly in a way which suits this particular motif.

The background is made from a piece of hardboard measuring 20 by 36 inches (50 by 90 cm) covered with hessian. Cut the fabric 3 to 4 inches (8-10 cm) larger than the board, fold the edges over the sides and glue them to the back. If you can't find the colour hessian you want, you can paint the board with a couple of coats of acrylic paint. We have used an egg-shell coloured background.

The stalk consists of two pieces of thick green cord, while the leaves are made of coloured twine of various kinds glued on as shewn in the photograph and figure 21. You will find it helps to cut paper shapes beforehand so that you get the right shape and size.

When it comes to sticking on the twine, you should spread a synthetic resin glue both on the backing and on the twine. Lay the shapes in place, holding the outlines firmly in place while you continue with the spirals. It may be necessary to press the board under a heavy object until the glue is dry.

The large flower should only be glued round the edges so that the centre is not pressed flat.

You can hang the picture up by glueing a piece of string with the ends unravelled to the back as in figure 22.

Baskets from simple weaving

You can make more than just flat objects on a weaving ring, like baskets, for example. You will need to dress the warp in a different way, and can use this same method if you want to make a larger mat than that shewn on page 68. Following this procedure you can use the whole length of the warp thread to weave on (see figure 23). The warp should be about twenty-eight times the diameter of the ring.

23. Dressing the loom 1. Note that this method gives you double the number of threads resulting from the method described on page 69 (though also double the number of threads in the centre). Note, too, that the web can be removed from the loom without cutting the warp at the edges. All you do is take the cord from the outer side of the ring and draw the warp through the holes.

22. Hanging the picture.

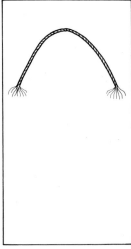

Dressing the warp 1. Since the warp thread is generally composed of fairly thick twine, it is handy to moisten the tip with glue and roll it till it is thinner. This will make it much easier to stick it up through a hole and back through the same hole. Tie the unrolled end of the thread to hole 1 so that there is a piece about 4 inches (10 cm) long hanging loose. Pass the thread from hole 1 to hole 14, through this, round a thick cord which runs round the outer side of the ring, as in figure 23, back through the same hole over to hole 2, through hole 2 round the cord and back through hole 2. Continue from there to

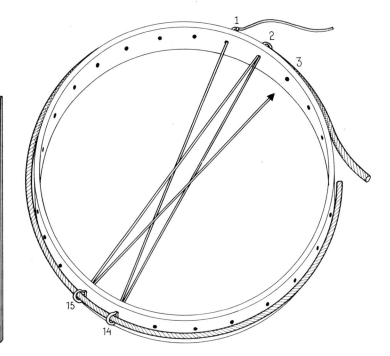

hole 15 and on to the end at hole 25. Then pass the thread in to the centre and start weaving as on the diagram on page 69.

The bottom of the basket is woven as already described until it measures about 6 inches (15 cm) across. Then start cross weaving as on page 70. Finally pull the thick cord on the outer side of the ring carefully out of the eyes in the warp and draw the warp threads through the holes in the ring. If the warp isn't stiff enough you can varnish whatever hasn't been woven before pulling it out of the holes. This makes the final rows of weaving easier.

As this method tends to make the middle section very thick it is wise to press the bottom under a damp cloth with a hot iron before continuing the cross weaving up the sides in the desired colours.

The advantage of cross weaving over other techniques is that it keeps the shape of the basket better. The work is finished off at the top by small loops in the warp thread. If you want a firmer basket you can varnish it one or more times with cellulose varnish and a thinner.

24. Dressing the loom 2. Here a small central ring has been inserted, with two extra strings to hold it in place until the warp is finished.

If the warp thread is thin enough to be doubled before insertion through the holes on the ring, thus forming a little eye on the outside, you can avoid having to draw the whole thread through but can just pass the eye and pull the warp thread tight. The same method can be used for dressing the loom as above, though in that case you will use both ends of the cord alternately on opposite sides of the ring. Both these methods can also be used when weaving on a cycle wheel.

These three baskets
have been woven on a
weaving ring following
various methods. They
are fun to make and
offer opportunities for
varying both pattern and
colour combination.

Dressing the warp 2. If you want the centre of the basket to be flatter you can dress the warp in the following way: attach a metal ring about 1 inch (2 - 3 cm) in diameter (or a ring glued together out of string) to the centre of the weaving ring by using extra threads; see diagram. Fasten one end of the warp thread to hole number 1 leaving enough of a loose end to reach the middle. Wind the warp round the ring in the middle out of one hole, round a cord and in the same hole as for the previous method. Continue this all the way round in the order hole 2 to hole 3 to hole 4 and so forth.

This method requires a high degree of accuracy as the central ring must stay exactly in the middle. If not, the basket will be lopsided.

When the warp is dressed and you have removed the extra threads attaching the ring you can start weaving over and under two threads in the colours available. This gives the spiral effect.

Note that the loose end of the warp should not be included in the weaving until the bottom is finished. Then you can untie the knot, pass the thread out through the hole and round the outer cord like the other threads.

You can fill out the central ring by darning.

If you want vertical stripes in the upright edge of the basket you should cross weave with two weft threads in different colours.

See the method described above.

You can use the same procedure with a cycle wheel loom.

Using a weaving ring to decorate a round box

You can use any round cardboard box as a basis for this, as long as it is not too big in relation to the weaving ring on which you are weaving a cover for the lid. (For the method, see pages 69 and 73.)

You can use coloured fishing yarn for both warp and weft, though a slightly stronger material is probably preferable.

See pages 69 and 74 for the actual weaving.

When the web is the same size as the lid you should glue it on before removing it from the weaving ring to prevent it coming undone.

Make sure that the woven work fits the edges of the lid exactly. When the glue has dried cut the warp at the holes and stick the threads down the sides of the lid cutting away any excess thread as in figure 25. Then bind round the sides right down to the bottom edge of the lid, applying plenty of glue to prevent the binding being pushed off.

Bind the box itself from the bottom up to the point reached by the lid.

The pattern on the surface of the lid is made on a weaving ring.

25. After sticking on the round piece of weave glue the warp ends down the sides of lid and bind over them right down to the lower edge.

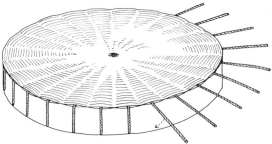

Weaving

Weaving with oddments of packing twine

The bag in photograph A was woven on a so-called plank loom. This technique produces a symmetical pattern and is therefore especially suited to the use of oddments, though you can also follow the instructions for weaving bags on page 86.

Apart from these there is an ordinary frame loom, but if you use this you should remember to fasten the beginning and end extra well as packing twine tends to have a mind of its own.

Reckon on about twenty-five warp threads to 4 inches (10 cm). The weft is oddments of twine from parcels. Various thicknesses and colours have been used, indeed anything which would contribute to the rustic look of the bag, unachievable with uniform materials.

Any very thin twine has been woven double while things like sisal which are really thick have been used singly. You can achieve a decorative zig-zag effect by twisting the sisal before you weave it in.

The oddments of twine should be long enough to fringe at the ends. Then both sides of the bag can be given a gay trim along the edges folded over at the top.

Before removing the work from the loom, sew a row of hem stitching along the edge to stop it coming undone and keep the fringing in place (see figure 26).

Join the bag down the sides and fold back the top. You can make a clasp by sewing a loop on one side and a toggle on the other.

Plait the twine to form a handle; you can make it any length you wish. Then fringe the ends and sew it on down the sides of the bag.

If you want to you can line the bag and strengthen it with buckram, a specially stiffened hessian designed for mounting fabric.

Variations on a theme

26. Securing the threads at the ends of the web.

With Bag B the warp is raffia while the weft thread consists of unbleached cotton yarn and sisal twine from parcels.

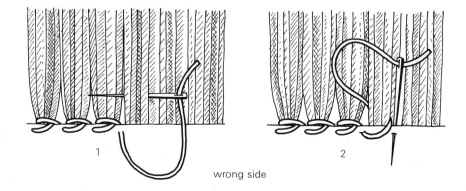

1   2

wrong side

Use plain weave throughout. The thicker thread, however, will give the weave a highly unusual effect as the raffia shows through. The same idea can be used for many other articles.

The back consists of plain raffia weaving. Sew a line of hem stitching along the bottom edge of the bag, as in the diagram, before taking the web off the loom. If you use the method demonstrated you will be able to keep the stitching firm.

Cut the sisal twine down the sides of the bag and sew a line of machine stitching along the edge to stop the twine slipping out.

Sew on the backpiece and turn down the top before attaching the lining. Knot a string handle from the sisal, making it as long or short as you wish, and fasten the bag at the top with a button and a loop of twine.

A: This bag is woven of oddments of twine from parcels, giving it an interesting variety of colour and texture.

B: You can achieve an interesting effect by combining materials as here where cotton yarn and sisal twine have been woven in a raffia warp.

Crossed weave

Bag

Cross woven fabric is a new discovery and as it is often used in conjunction with fishing yarn it seems reasonable to include it in this book. This material can be put to many different uses and is convenient to work with since the holes through which it is embroidered stand out very clearly.

Crossed woven fabric is available in several colours, including white, beige and grey. The choice of colour should be determined by the degree to which the pattern will show up against the fabric.

It can also be used to great advantage with thick cotton or wool yarn or with raffia.

Materials. Make the bag from a piece of crossed woven fabric measuring 15 by 22 inches (38 by 55 cm). You will also need a piece of lining material the same size and a piece of iron-on interlining double the size. About 4 ounces (112 grams) of undyed fishing yarn and a wooden handle.

Crossed woven fabric embroidered with fishing twine make an attractive and decorative combination. The unusual wooden handle adds a distinctive quality.

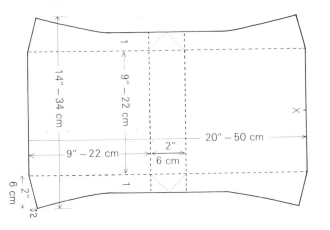

27. Pattern for the bag. X marks the centre where you should start the embroidery.

To make the bottom firm you can use a piece of glazed cardboard or doubled buckram measuring about 2 by 9 inches (6 by 22 cm). For the embroidery you will need a canvas needle, with a very large eye but no point.

The embroidery. There may be slight variations in the weave but the fabric usually consists of narrow threads going in one direction and slightly wider threads in the other. In this case we have embroidered under the wide thread (see figure 28).

28. Pattern suggestion.

29. Diagram for the bag.

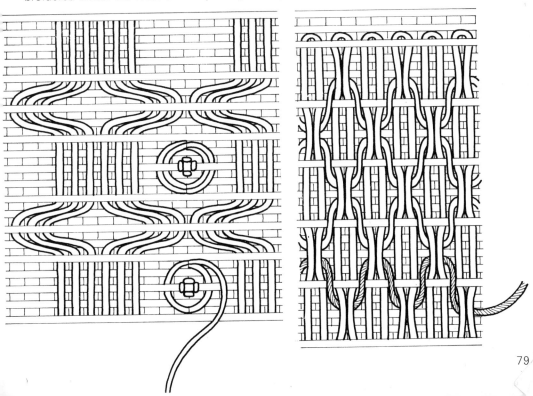

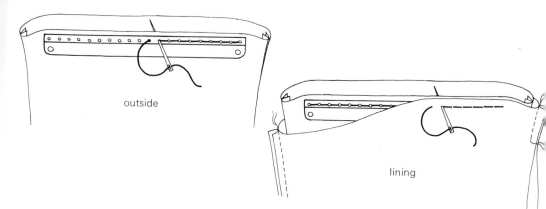

outside

lining

30. Attaching the handle.

31. Attaching the lining.

Start the embroidery at the centre point of one end, marked X on the pattern (figure 27). First sew a long row of zig-zag stitches and then fill in the 'flowers'. These are made by back-stitching a square over the centre thread of the panel.

Then bring the needle out one hole down and sew twice round the original square with both rounds in the same holes. Carry on to the next flower without breaking the thread (see figure 29).

Continue the embroidery out to the sides until it reaches exactly the same width as the wooden handles. Then change to a flat stitch until the work is the required measurement, in this case about 14 inches (34 cm) wide (see photograph).

Backing the embroidery. Press the work on the wrong side and attach the interlining so that it fits the embroidery exactly. The corners should be proper right angles. Then iron on the first layer of interlining. It is very important that the corners should be at ninety degrees. You may find it necessary to pull at the embroidery to get it right. If you don't make the initial work neat you will not achieve a very good end product.

Cut out the board or the double layer of buckram for the bottom according to the pattern. Lay this in place and then iron on the second layer of interlining.

Fold the embroidery right sides together and join the two sides working from the top as far down as the bottom gusset allows. Turn right side out, fold in at the bottom and join the bottom part of the side seams and the piece you have folded in with a close line of stitching on the outside.

Lay the piece of wood with the small holes uppermost on the right side of the embroidery and sew it firmly and flatly to the top edge of the bag using a strong thread. See figure 30 and the photograph and note that the top edge of the embroidery is mounted inside the bag.

Join the lining down one side and for 2 inches (5 cm) down the other side, making sure that the length and breadth are the same as that of the main body of the bag. Pull this over the bag, right sides together, taking care not to wrinkle the embroidery. Sew it firmly

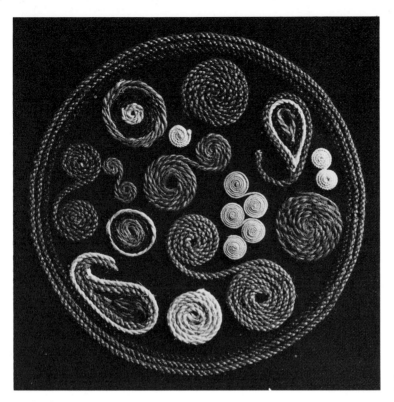

A wall decoration in hessian.

to the inner side of the wooden handle, pushing your needle right through to include the embroidery, the wooden mount and the lining in each stitch (see figure 31). Sew the lining and the outer fabric together over the frame so that the embroidery is drawn over the ends of the wood. With patience you can now ease the lining over the bag through the opening in the side. Then when the lining is in place you can join this opening.

Make the chain for the handle by knotting or crocheting and make the join at the two ends as indiscernible as possible.

Wall decorations

A string picture

On page 70 you can see how to make a picture with the use of a weaving ring. But it is possible to make pictures or wall hangings in many different ways. If you experiment with various materials you will doubtless come up with further ideas.

This wall hanging is based on a stretcher, about 20 by 20 inches (48 by 48 cm). Cut a piece of black hessian about 26 inches (62 cm) square and glue it onto the frame.

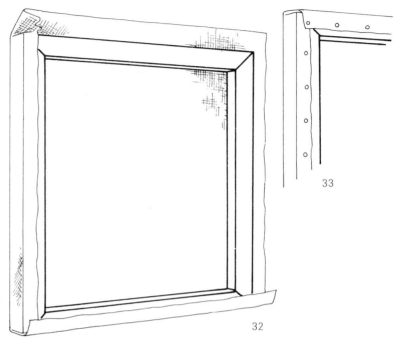

33

32

32 and 33. Fasten the material to the back of the frame. Don't cut away the corners but fold them neatly and nail down.

When it is stuck firmly onto the back of the frame as in figure 32, bang in small tacks to hold it in place. Don't cut the material at the corners but fold it as in figure 33.

The inner ring has a diameter of 13 inches (32 cm) and it is best to start with this. You can work out the correct position by laying a round object of the same diameter in the centre of the frame and drawing or tacking round the edge.

Attach a piece of twine round this circle, either with glue or with tiny stitches. We have used sisal clothes-line dyed dark grey, light grey and reddish brown.

Then coil and wind shapes in whichever materials and colours will suit. We have kept to the three colours already mentioned plus white. The fact that we have, however, used many different kinds of materials is what gives work of this sort such a vivid effect.

You should dab on some glue between each spiral you make but make sure that it is spread thinly. Stick a pin in to prevent the coil unrolling before the glue has dried.

When you have collected a suitable number of shapes, experiment with the layout so that you can get a general idea of how the separate parts of the picture should be arranged and where you may need to add something.

Then, once everything is ready, you can stick each thing in the place you have decided and finish by adding the two outer rings of light grey and red sisal.

Weaving a picture in sisal

The art work in the photograph on page 81 is made of coloured sisal in various thicknesses and produced actually on the frame. Hammer nails $\frac{1}{2}$ inch (1 cm) apart into the back of the frame, though you must be careful that the nails don't go through the frame. You can use a stretcher, obtainable at an artists' materials shop.

You should use nails with really large heads. If you start by glueing a strip of squared paper onto the frame where the nails are to go, you will find it easier to space them at an equal distance from each other (see figure 34).

Dress the loom with fishing yarn or some other kind of twine, by either passing it over two nails as here or, if you want a closer warp, over one nail which will double the number of warp threads.

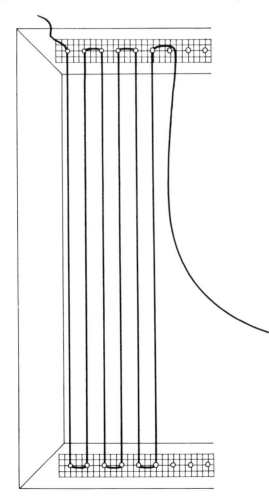

34. Preparing a weaving frame for picture weaving. Use squared paper to help you bang in the nails at regular intervals. If you want a closer warp, draw the thread over one nail on each side, alternately.

The picture is made by playing around with shapes and colours, weaving over and under the warp with your fingers on the right side of the work. Use partly thick yarn and partly oddments of thinner materials.

Some of the ends form part of the picture as the tails of imaginary fishes. The other ends are on the back of the work, in those cases where they could not be included in the weaving.

Sew on beads for the fishes' eyes.

Obviously fish is only one example for this method; the same technique can be used for many other ideas so that you can work with oddments of twine in an interesting way.

Decorations made as group work

The pictures in the photographs have been assembled from the work of a group in an old people's home. But there is no reason why the joys of working with special effects of this kind should be

You can achieve the coarse-textured effect called for by picture weaving in many ways, for example, by interlacing only part of the warp and allowing the remaining threads to stay open.

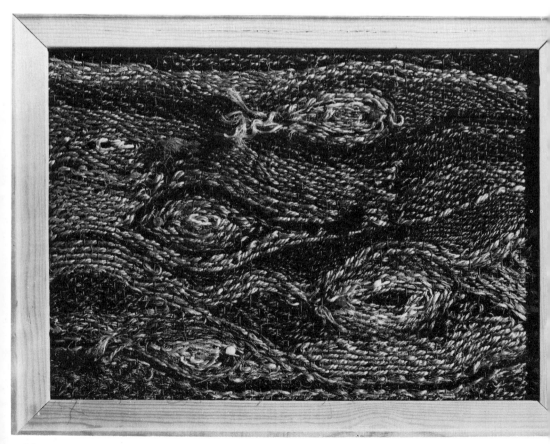

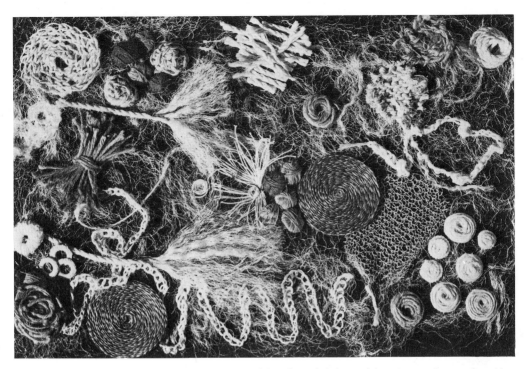

confined to the elderly. You could get a lot of fun from joining with your children, of whatever age, to produce similar pictures.

In this case we have made the background from a flat piece of wood painted black, on which the various items have been glued. These may follow your own wants and abilities.

Glue on unravelled sisal cord as a base. The shapes are made of odd pieces of knitting or crochet, coiled cord or string crocheted in chains which have either been stuck on in piles or just trimmed and assembled together. In several cases we have grouped small balls of yarn together in circles or clusters and then glued them on.

We have also used rings of twine oversewn with the buttonhole stitch.

The final composition and glueing on requires a certain sense of balance and should be considered carefully. Obviously it is preferable if the artists who have contributed have their say too.

Work of this kind also affords an opportunity of using materials which are quite different (sea shells, stone and twigs for example) and which will look attractive in conjunction with cord and twine.

Decoration produced by group work. The black surface is overlaid with unravelled sisal cord glued in place before the other details are added.

An unconventional way of making a bag by darning symmetrically with coloured twine.

35. Darning a handle of a strip woven on a ribbon loom into the sides of the bag. In the photograph the handle has been made of a strip of webbing.

Simple weaving on a rack

Bag

Here is a highly unconventional method of making such articles as bags. Make a rack from four ½ by 1 inch (1 by 2 cm) pieces of wood, two of them 10 inches (24 cm) long and two 16 inches (40 cm), though naturally you can use other lengths.

Join the wood to form a rectangle and glue with Araldite. A couple of thin tacks can be hammered in each corner to make the joins more secure. The narrower sides of the wood should be turned upwards (see figure 35).

Dressing the warp. Wind thin jute twine or a smooth material like fishing yarn round the rack. Tie the warp thread to the frame and wind right round the outer side along the longer sides.

We have made the warp about 8 inches (20 cm) deep by winding twenty-four threads equally spaced. Cross weave along the edge of the wood as in figure 36 to keep the warp threads equidistant.

Start at the top and weave down along one side of the wood. Then let the threads run over the bottom to make extra warp threads before continuing up the other side as in figure 37.

Do the same thing on the other side of the frame.

Darning in the weft. For this you should use a very large needle threaded with double sisal twine or whatever you wish to use.

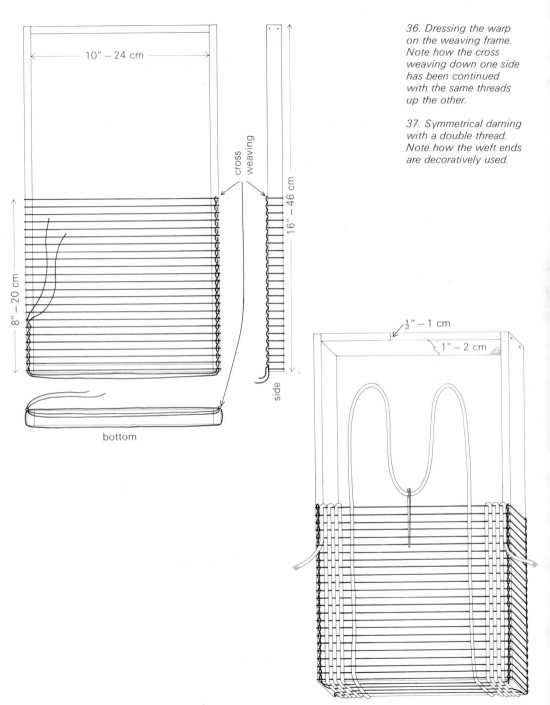

10" – 24 cm

8" – 20 cm

16" – 46 cm

cross
weaving

side

bottom

½" – 1 cm

1" – 2 cm

36. Dressing the warp
on the weaving frame.
Note how the cross
weaving down one side
has been continued
with the same threads
up the other.

37. Symmetrical darning
with a double thread.
Note how the weft ends
are decoratively used.

To avoid fastening in the ends, you can start interlacing the weft a little way down the warp. Then, later, you can unravel the ends of the threads to make a tasselled edge. Weave upwards, placing each end of the thread out to opposite sides, and continue down the middle, through the warp threads on the bottom of the frame and up the other side.

Carry on pushing the threads out to the sides so that you have a symmetrical pattern, and on both sides at once.

When you have finished the weft thread or want to change to another colour, it is best to piece the threads where the tassel is to be.

You may find it hard to pull through the last thread in the middle, but you can probably manage it if you push the other threads firmly out to the sides. Then you can ease them back towards the middle when you have finished.

Finally, pull the bag off the frame.

There are various ways in which you can make the handle.

1. Buy webbing in a matching colour from a saddler and fold it into three thicknesses. Sew down the edge. Then insert it carefully over and under the warp threads down one side. Insert the other end of the webbing down the other side in the same way. Overlap the webbing at the bottom and join to form a firm base.

2. Weave a handle on a ribbon loom using the same materials as for the bag and leaving enough free threads at each end to weave into the warp threads at the sides of the bag and form a tassel at the bottom.

It is easy enough to fit the bag together when, as here, you have used webbing for the sides and the handle.

There are various other possibilities as far as making the handles is concerned. Try working out one for yourself.

Various other techniques

Basket weaving

If you take a needlework basket and give it a strong handle you can transform it into a roomy shopping basket. Since the paper string used for the weaving is dyed at home, you can decide which colours you want yourself.

Materials. The bottom consists of a wooden base about one third of an inch (8-9 mm) thick with holes drilled at intervals of about three eighths of an inch (1 cm) round the edge. These holes should be quite deep and big enough to take cane an eighth of an inch ($2\frac{1}{2}$ mm) thick at a tight fit. The wood in the model measures about $6\frac{1}{2}$ inches (17 cm) across and is furnished with thirty-six holes (see figure 38).

For a pattern of vertical stripes you need an even number of holes.

Make the stakes from 14 inch (36 cm) lengths of eighth of an inch ($2\frac{1}{2}$ mm) cane. You will also need some soft twine, jute would do, for the first few rows and then paper string in white and two other colours. We have used black and brown (see page 53 on dyeing). In the model the stakes have been coloured brown.

Procedure. Soak the cane stakes for about ten minutes and then insert them in the holes. To make the stakes bend upwards you should start by tightly weaving about twelve double rows with two threads of jute twine. If you double over the thread at the beginning you will avoid having odd ends. Then continue weaving with heavy duty paper string, still using two threads because of the even number of stakes. If, for example, you use one white and one brown thread, this will result in a vertical stripe (see figure 39).

When you have reached the required height, dampen the cane thoroughly making sure that the paper string doesn't get wet. Then weave the three rows which form the edge so that it lies inside the basket.

First row. Take one stake, pass it behind the stake to the right and into the basket. Look closely at figure 40. Continue in the same way until you reach the last stake which should be inserted in the first curve.

38. Stakes stuck in the holes in the bottom.

39. By weaving with two threads in different colours, you can make a pattern of vertical stripes so long as there is an even number of stakes.

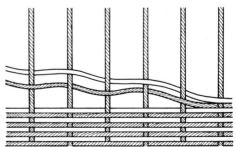

89

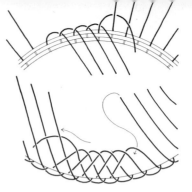

40. First row of edging.

41. Second row of edging.

Second row. Weave from right to left. Take one stake, pass it under the first stake to the left, over the next one and down into the basket. Repeat this process all the way round, finishing by weaving the last stake down into the first two stakes in the row which can be slightly loosened (figure 41).

Third row. Weave in exactly the same way as for the second row using the cane which now lies inside the basket.

Any surplus cane can be cut off with pliers. But be careful not to trim them so closely that the ends can slip out.

If you want to make the basket stiffer you can varnish it.

Masks

42. Dressing the warp in the weaving ring with sennit knots. Note the order in which they are tied.

You can use a weaving ring to make many different kinds of things. In this case it has been used to produce masks. If you don't own a weaving ring you can use a circle of wire, from a lampshade for example.

The instructions given here are for a weaving ring.

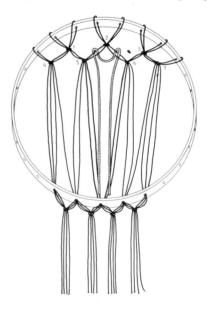

Over the centuries many different materials and techniques have been used in the production of masks. Here we have employed a crochet and darning technique respectively with various kinds of twine.

Procedure. Thread pieces of heavy twine, like sisal, through the top eight holes on the ring. When double, each piece should measure about twice the diameter of the ring.

43. Sennit knot.

Tie the threads together from above in sennits, which are reef knots round two cords (figure 43), following the order 1 to 7 marked on figure 42.

Then thread the ends through the holes at the bottom of the ring and tie them tightly. Add a piece of double jute twine in the middle as shewn.

Taking brown jute twine, or any colour you wish, darn backwards and forwards between the knots at the top so that they are partly covered. You could also use other kinds of yarn. Continue in this way down to the eyes which are woven over six threads in white, though you should add a dark spot inside (see figure 44).

Continue weaving down the face omitting the double jute thread inserted in the middle. This will later be used as the basis for knotting a protruding nose in jute, with the ends tucked in the back of the work and held in place with glue. Weave the mouth over five threads, again with a darker section in the middle.

When the mask reaches a suitable size, draw the warp ends out of the holes at the bottom of the ring and knot two or three rows with them. You can then trim them to the required length and unravel the twine to form a beard.

If you want to remove the mask from the ring (though it will

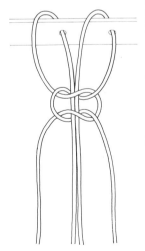

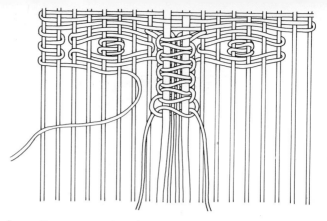

44. Weaving in the eyes and knotting the nose.

make quite an attractive decoration if hung on the wall with the ring still attached) you should glue the knots before cutting them off at the holes. Then fringe out the ends. You can also do as we have, and leave the mask on the ring with a couple of extra pieces of unravelled twine set in at the top to make the hair.

Crocheted mask

45. Diagrammatic picture of the crocheted mask.

This crocheted mask has been inspired by Indian raffia masks. The one in the picture has been made of jute, with white sisal for the hair and beard round the edge.

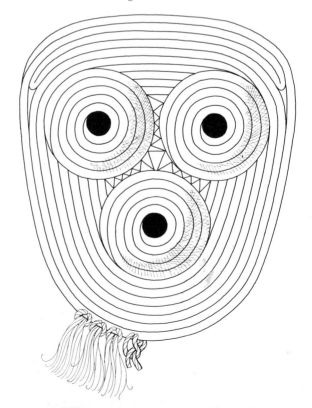

It is impossible to give precise instructions as to how to crochet the mask, so we shall merely describe the general procedure.

The two eye pieces and mouth are made by starting with a circle of eight to ten chains.

Continue in double crochet putting the hook through both loops of the chain. As you work outwards make the shapes convex so that the mask looks more animated. After crocheting five or six rounds sew the three pieces together as in figure 45 and continue with the crochet right the way round.

Adjust the crochet to make the shape you require. You may find it necessary to crochet some extra stitches where the three circles have been joined.

Crochet backwards and forwards across the top a few times. Then when the desired shape has been reached add a fringe of unravelled sisal twine round the edge as in figure 46.

Set a piece of thick jute twine in between the eyes and knot over this to form a sturdy nose which has been added to give the mask a distinctive expression.

There are great opportunities for variation on this basic shape.

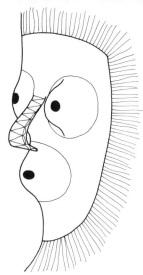

46. The eyes and mouth are crocheted so that they curve in towards the middle. The nose is also separately shaped.

The technique used for these 'kites' or 'friendly eyes' as they are called has been practised through the ages, and was known in Peru. They make ideal decorations, either in a window or on the wall.

93

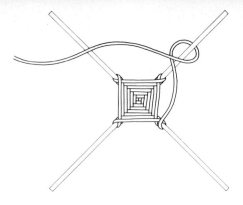

47. Binding two crossed sticks

'Kites'

These two bright 'kites' are fun to make and by no means difficult. You may already be familiar with the technique from making small, similar kites wound in wool. They can be used to decorate a window or wall or assembled into a mobile.

The large flag is made of two wooden garden stakes (not bamboo) sawn to the required length.

Join them into a cross with a thin, strong thread like fishing yarn at the intersection and then start binding outwards with twine (see figure 47).

When you change colours fasten the two ends with glue and wind the thread over them.

Gradually, as the work grows, you can start using some thicker and firmer string, though be careful to keep it flat and even.

We have used dark turquoise and yellowy green shades for the large flag but if you dye the twine yourself you will be able to choose from the whole spectrum.

The smaller flag is made in the same way as the large one, in this case in red and orange. Instead of the garden stakes, however, you will need a pair of small, flat sticks. Louvre slats will do or a couple of pieces of split cane.

Lampshade

The lampshade in the photograph allows you to have both a strong light underneath it and a subdued glow in the rest of the room. You can make it in any size you wish, even large enough to stand on the floor.

Ours is 12 inches (30 cm) high and about 25 inches (63 cm) round. The fabric is woven on a small loom, 12 inches (30 cm) wide. Both the warp and the weft are of fishing yarn. You will also need some blind slats or louvre slats about 14 inches (35 cm) long. The web is about 11 inches (27 cm) wide, with the slats overlapping it.

You can buy the metal rings for the lamps in large stores and craft shops. Various sizes are available and it is best to buy the rings beforehand so that you know the exact measurement of the circumference before you start weaving. You will then be able to adjust the web accordingly.

The lamp throws a good light down over the table, while the outline of the wooden slats on the shade creates an unusually cosy atmosphere.

The set consists of two rings of the same size which can only be used when the material is stiff enough to keep the height of the lampshade without support.

The top ring also has a holder for an electric light fitting.

The slats are woven into the warp in ones and twos with about eight weft threads between them.

Mounting. If you have a sewing machine which can make zig-zag stitches, it is as well to run a line of close stitching at both ends to stop the weave coming undone. Otherwise you can oversew by hand.

Try to ensure that the seam joining the fabric falls under a slat so that it can't be seen when the light is on.

Sew the edges of the woven fabric to the rings and adjust the sticks so that they are even.

If the light bulb shines too brightly through the shade you can cut a piece of cartridge paper, in white or cream, and glue it to fit exactly inside the shade. If you then push it up into position, you probably won't need to glue it to the shade.